GCSE Edexcel 360Science
Extension Science
The Workbook

This book is for anyone doing **GCSE Edexcel Extension Science Units**.

It's full of **tricky questions**... each one designed to make you **sweat** — because that's the only way you'll get any **better**.

There are questions to see **what facts** you know. There are questions to see how well you can **apply those facts**. And there are questions to see what you know about **how science works**.

It's also got some daft bits in to try and make the whole experience at least vaguely entertaining for you.

What CGP is all about

Our sole aim here at CGP is to produce the highest quality books — carefully written, immaculately presented and dangerously close to being funny.

Then we work our socks off to get them out to you — at the cheapest possible prices.

Contents

C3 Topic 4 — Chemistry Working for Us

P3 Topic 5 — Particles in Action

P3 Topic 6 — Medical Physics

Published by Coordination Group Publications Ltd.

Editors:
Ellen Bowness, Katherine Craig, Gemma Hallam, Sarah Hilton, Kate Houghton, Kate Redmond, Julie Wakeling, Sarah Williams.

Contributors:
Michael Aicken, Mike Bossart, Steve Coggins, Mike Dagless, James Foster, Derek Harvey, Jason Howell, Barbara Mascetti, Jim Wilson, Chris Workman.

ISBN: 978 1 84762 331 7

With thanks to Laura Stoney for the copyright research.

Data used to construct pie chart on page 57 from "Concise Dictionary of Chemistry" edited by Daintith, J (1986). By permission of Oxford University Press. www.oup.com

Every effort has been made to locate copyright holders and obtain permission to reproduce sources. For those sources where it has been difficult to trace the originator of the work, we would be grateful for information. If any copyright holder would like us to make an amendment to the acknowledgements, please notify us and we will gladly update the book at the next reprint. Thank you.

Groovy website: www.cgpbooks.co.uk

Printed by Elanders Hindson Ltd, Newcastle upon Tyne.
Jolly bits of clipart from CorelDRAW®

Microorganisms and Food

Q1 Complete the passage about **yoghurt making** by filling in the gaps using the words below.

cooled   ferment   flavours   clot   pasteurised   lactic acid   bacteria   incubated

To make yoghurt, milk is *pasteurised* to kill off any unwanted microorganisms, then *cooled*. Next, a starter culture of *bacteria* is added and the mixture is *incubated*. The bacteria *ferment* the lactose sugar into *lactic acid*. This causes the milk to *clot* and form yoghurt. *Flavours* such as fruit are then sometimes added.

Q2 Number these steps in the manufacture of **soy sauce** to give the correct order.

2 fermentation by *Aspergillus*   *6* pasteurisation

5 filtering   *3* fermentation by yeast

1 soya beans and roasted wheat are mixed   *4* fermentation by *Lactobacillus*

Q3 Scientists did an experiment into the effectiveness of **stanol esters** in lowering people's **blood cholesterol**. They asked two groups of 100 people each to use a special spread instead of butter. Group A's spread was based on vegetable oil. Group B's spread was exactly the same, except that it contained large amounts of stanol esters. The cholesterol levels of each group were measured before the start of the experiment, and again after six months. The results are shown in the table.

	Group A / units	Group B / units
Mean blood cholesterol at start	6.3	6.4
Mean blood cholesterol after 6 mths	6.1	5.5

a) Explain the purpose of Group A.

to see if there was difference between to show the effect of normal vegetable oil on the groups cholesterol which would be compared to veg oil with stanol esters in it.

b) Why did the scientists use 100 people in each group?

to get a more accurate result

c) What precautions should the scientists have taken when choosing people for this experiment, to make sure that their results were valid?

they should have made sure nobody had extremely high, or extremeley low cholesterol, they should have had around about the same levels

d) Why is it necessary to measure the blood cholesterol before the experiment as well as at the end?

so you can evaluate the change if there is one.

e) Explain how bacteria are involved in making spreads such as that used by group B.

Stanol esters are put into those spreads Produced naturally in plants and commercially formed by using bacteria to convert sterols into stanols.

Microorganisms and Food

Q4 Different substances are added to foods for different reasons.
Draw lines to match each of these **food additives** to its **function**.

a) Chymosin — sweetener

b) Fructose — flavouring

c) MSG — preservative

d) Vitamin C — clotting agent

(matching lines drawn connecting: Chymosin→clotting agent, Fructose→sweetener, MSG→flavouring, Vitamin C→preservative)

Q5 The Complacent Cow Company makes **cheese** from cow's milk using an **enzyme** that comes from **genetically modified yeast**. They claim that they "make cheese without cruelty to animals".

a) Name the enzyme that the Complacent Cow Company uses. ..... Chymosin .....

b) Describe briefly how yeasts can be made to produce this enzyme.

Cells from the lining of a calf's stomach which produce thes enzyme are isolated, and put into yeast cells to be grown commercially.

c) Explain why the Complacent Cow Company's cheese might be popular with vegetarians, but cheese from other companies might not be.

because the enzyme used to make the cheese is obtained from the lining of a calf's stomach, then isolated, making it vegetarian cheese

Q6 A sweet manufacturer uses an enzyme produced by **yeast** to convert **sucrose** into **fructose**.

a) Name the enzyme involved in this process.

invertase.

b) Explain the purpose of converting sucrose into fructose.

So less sugar is needed for the same amount of sweetness, saving the manufacturers money, and enabling them to produce lower calorie sweet foods.

Q7 Consider the **commercial manufacture** of the **food products** listed in the box below.

| carrageenan | citric acid | fructose | soy sauce | stanols | yoghurt |

From this list, choose the product or products:

a) used as a preservative. citric acid

b) depending on fungi for production. Soy sauce

c) depending on bacteria for production. yoghurt

d) not requiring microorganisms for production. carrageenan

Diet and Obesity

Q1   Complete the following sentences to show the **functions** in the body of different **nutrients**.

a)   Protein is needed for ...growth & repair of tissue..... and ...for energy in emergencies.

b)   Carbohydrates provide much of your ......energy.............................

c)   Fats are used to form cell ....membranes.............. and ....steroid........... hormones.

Q2   **Kwashiorkor** is a condition caused by lack of **protein** in the diet.

Why is this condition most common in poorer developing countries?

.....because....high-fibre...foods...are...scarce...or...too...expensive.....................

Q3   **Vitamins** and **minerals** are two **essential nutrients** needed in the diet. Explain why each of the following examples are needed, and what the health consequences could be if they are lacking.

a)   **Vitamin C** is needed for ...maintain...healthy....connective..tissue....................

A lack of vitamin C could lead to ...scurvy.............................

b)   **Iron** is needed for ...producing....heamoglobin...for...the...blood...cells...........

A lack of iron could lead to ...anemia....................

Q4   **Fifty** men and **fifty** women were asked whether they thought they were **obese**.
Each was then given a medical examination to **check** whether they were actually obese.

	Thought they were obese	Actually obese
No. of women	9	16
No. of men	5	11

a)   What percentage of women in this survey were obese? .....16%..

b)   What are the most common **causes** of obesity in developed countries?

...too...much...fats,...carbs...and...protein...in...their...diet...-malnutrition.....

c)   Is an obesity study based on data from **questionnaires** likely to be accurate? Explain your answer.

...no,...it...is...likely...to...be...unaccurate...because...people........
...would...possibly...not...to be...truthful..........

d)   Underline any health problems in the list below that have been linked to obesity.

(heart disease)   (hepatitis)   influenza   (cancers)   scurvy   (diabetes)

___

Top Tips: Don't forget, **malnutrition** is when the diet you eat isn't balanced — which includes eating **too much**, as well as too little or not enough of certain things.

4

Genetically Modifying Plants

Q1 Use the words provided to fill in the blanks in the passage below.

bacteria   herbicide   insecticide   plants   vector

Agrobacterium tumefaciens and *Bacillus thuringiensis* are both ...*bacteria*... that can be used in biotechnology. *Agrobacterium tumefaciens* can be used as a ...*vector*... to insert a gene for ...*herbicide*... resistance into plants. *Bacillus thuringiensis* produces a natural ...*insecticide*... and the gene for this can be cut out and inserted into ...*plants*...

Q2 **Famine** and **malnutrition** have various causes, and **biotechnology** can help to find solutions for some of them. Look at the descriptions of **genetically modified plants** below, and in each case say which **cause of famine** or malnutrition it could provide a solution to.

e.g. Plants that can tolerate water loss.   *drought*

a) Plants that can fix their own nitrogen.

b) Plants that contain extra vitamins.

c) Plants that produce their own insecticide.

Q3 These are some statements that different people made about **GM plants**. In each case, say whether they are making an argument **for** or **against** GM technology.

a) *"Genes newly inserted into crop plants, for example for pest-resistance, may spread to nearby wild plants."* — Gregory Greene, conservationist.   *against*

b) **"Some people could develop allergic reactions to foods that have been genetically modified."** — Jermaine Eaton, nutritionist.   *against*

c) *"We can produce rice plants containing toxins that are harmful to locusts but not to people."* — Veronica Speedwell, biotechnology consultant.   *for*

d) **"By using herbicide-resistant crops on my land, I can kill all the weeds in my field with a single dose of all-purpose herbicide."** — Ed Jones, farmer.   *for*

e) *"Investing in improving traditional agricultural methods will improve yields more than investment in GM technology."* — Abigail Singh, relief worker.   *against*

Q4 Some stages in the production of a **herbicide-resistant maize plant** are listed below. Put the stages in the correct order.

A The herbicide-resistance gene is inserted into *Agrobacterium tumefaciens*.

B Infected cells from maize are grown in a medium containing herbicide.

C The gene that makes a wild corn plant resistant to herbicide is identified.

D *Agrobacterium tumefaciens* is allowed to infect a maize plant.

E The herbicide-resistance gene is cut out from a wild corn plant.

Order: *C   E   A   D   B*

Genetically Modifying Plants

Q5 Unicourt Biotech, an American company, has developed a new **GM rice** that gives a **higher yield** than ordinary rice and which is also **resistant to diseases.**

Ruritasia is a poor island in South-East Asia. The rice would grow well there, but some of the local farmers **don't** want to use it.

a) Why might it be good for the people of Ruritasia if they used the GM rice?

....

....

b) The people of Ruritasia have several different objections to the use of GM rice. Explain each of the objections given below:

i) It's a danger to people's health.

....

ii) It's a danger to local habitats.

....

iii) It causes dependence on a foreign company.

....

....

c) If the climate in Ruritasia changed, resulting in lack of rain, what kind of GM crop could be used?

....

Q6 **Golden rice** was developed in order to increase the amount of **vitamin A** that could be obtained from a rice crop. It is estimated that a person would only have to eat **144 g** of golden rice per day in order to receive the recommended daily allowance of vitamin A, compared with **2.3 kg** of natural basmati rice.

a) Golden rice does not actually contain much more vitamin A than basmati rice. Explain how Golden rice increases the amount of vitamin A that a person receives.

....

....

b) It has been suggested that Golden rice would be very useful as a crop in developing countries. Explain why it might be particularly useful in such countries.

....

....

Genetically Modifying Plants

Q7 A crop plant had been genetically modified to make it **resistant to herbicides**. Some people were **concerned** that, as a result, wild grasses growing nearby might also become resistant to herbicides. Scientists decided to check whether this had happened.

The scientists sprayed herbicide onto 100 plants in an area next to the GM crop, and onto 100 plants from a second area far away from the GM crop. The results are shown in the table.

Number of grass plants dying after spraying	
In area next to GM crop	In area far away from GM crop
83	85

a) Explain the reason for testing a group of plants that had not been growing near the GM crop.

....

b) How could the scientists have made the results of this experiment **more reliable**?

....

c) The scientists decided that there was no significant difference between the two groups of plants. Explain whether you agree or disagree with this conclusion.

....

....

d) If the scientists are right in their conclusion, does this prove that the concerns about genes for resistance spreading are unfounded? Explain your answer.

....

....

....

e) If wild grasses become resistant to herbicides, what **problems** might this cause?

....

....

f) Crop plants can be genetically modified so that they grow better under various conditions, or so that their nutritional value is improved. Suggest **two** other reasons why a crop might be modified.

....

....

Top Tips: If GM organisms **don't** cause any unexpected problems, then all's fine and dandy. But if it turns out that they **do**, it could be a problem, as they're **already** being used in some countries.

New Treatments — Drugs

Q1 The table shows some different **drugs** that can be extracted from **plants** and their **uses**. Fill in the blanks to complete it.

DRUG	EXTRACTED FROM	USES
artemisinin	*Artemisia annua* plant	
salicin		painkiller
	Pacific yew tree	
quinine		anti-malarial

Q2 When companies produce a **new drug**, they are allowed to **patent** it. Then they can control the **price** at which they sell it. Some people think that this system is a good idea, but others don't.

For each of the quotes below, say whether you think the person is **for** or **against** the patent system.

a) "It costs millions of pounds to do the research needed to create a new drug."   ....

b) "Drug companies are making money out of people's suffering."   ....

c) "Less economically developed countries can't afford to buy essential new drugs."...........................

d) "Companies need an incentive to invest in the development of new drugs."   ....

e) "Companies that make copies of new drugs can provide them more cheaply."   ....

Q3 The graph shows the amount of **money** spent on buying **drugs** by the health services of two countries with similar population sizes.

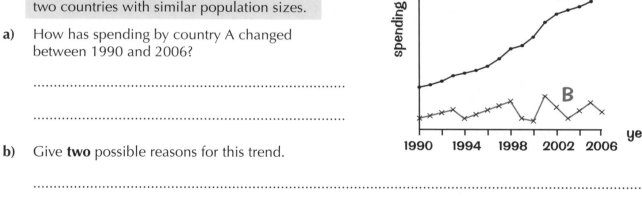

a) How has spending by country A changed between 1990 and 2006?

....

....

b) Give **two** possible reasons for this trend.

....

c) Suggest why the spending by country **B** does not show a similar trend.

....

d) Explain how abandoning the patent system for new drugs might help country B.

....

....

e) Explain why abandoning the patent system might **not** be a good idea for people in either country.

....

New Treatments — Using Genetics

Q1   **Genetically modified bacteria** can be made to produce **human insulin**. There are several **advantages** of this over using insulin from animals. Explain each of the advantages given below.

a)   Safety ....

b)   Quantity ....

c)   Economic advantages ....

d)   Suitability for vegetarians and vegans ....

e)   Quality ....

Q2   Use the words provided in the box to fill in the blanks in the passage below.

design   genome   genomics   medicine   predispose   prevent

> The complete genetic make-up of an organism is its ....
> The study of this is called ...., and it could be useful in
> ...., to develop treatments. Some people have genes
> which .... them to certain diseases. Identifying these
> genes in a person may help to .... the diseases ever
> developing. One day, it may also help doctors to ....
> specific drugs which suit an individual patient's particular genetic make-up.

Q3   It is known that if a woman is carrying a certain **gene**, her chances of developing **breast cancer** before the age of 45 are **significantly higher** than the chances of a woman without this gene developing breast cancer before this age.

a)   If a woman is a carrier of this gene:

  i)   suggest two advantages of her knowing that she has the gene.

  ....

  ....

  ii)   suggest one disadvantage of her knowing.

  ....

b)   Explain how knowing more about this gene could help scientists improve the treatment available.

....

....

....

Reproductive Technology

Q1 Read the paragraph below, and then answer the questions that follow.

> Mr and Mrs Reuben can't have a baby, because Mrs Reuben is unable to carry a child. However, Mrs Artemis agrees that she will carry a child for them. Mr and Mrs Reuben provide the sperm and eggs, and fertilisation is carried out _in vitro_. Then two healthy embryos are implanted into Mrs Artemis' uterus. Nine months later, Mrs Artemis gives birth to a baby girl.

a) Who is the baby's:

   i) genetic mother? ....

   ii) surrogate mother? ....

b) Explain what is meant by _in vitro_ fertilisation.

   ....

c) Two healthy embryos were implanted into Mrs Artemis' uterus.

   i) Suggest why two embryos were implanted.

   ....

   ii) Until quite recently, up to five embryos would usually be implanted in a single IVF treatment. Suggest why this is now not allowed.

   ....

Q2 The table shows the number of **IVF treatments** in a European country between 1990 and 2006.

YEAR	NO. OF TREATMENTS
1990	0
1992	2
1994	16
1996	55
1998	186
2000	348
2002	620
2004	740
2006	760

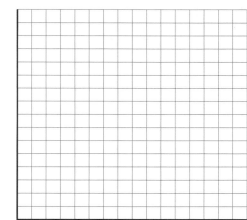

a) Plot this information on the grid provided.

b) Describe how the number of IVF treatments has changed during this time.

....

c) Suggest a possible reason for the trend that you have described.

....

Reproductive Technology

Q3   Mr and Mrs Partridge have a child aged three, called Jason, who needs a **liver transplant**. They want to have a second child using **IVF**, and to choose an embryo with a **tissue match** for Jason, with the hope that the second child will be able to donate part of their liver.

a)   Explain why IVF (compared to normal fertilisation) makes it easier to have a child that will be a tissue match.

....

....

b)   The only reason for using the IVF procedure would be to find a tissue match for Jason.

i)   What would happen to embryos produced by the procedure that do not have matching tissues?

....

ii)   Explain why some people feel that this would not be justified.

....

....

iii)   Explain why other people feel that the procedure would be justified.

....

....

Q4   In the UK, it is legal to **screen** IVF embryos for **genetic disorders**, but it isn't usually legal to select the **sex** of the baby, and it isn't legal to screen them for other characteristics, such as eye colour.

a)   Give two reasons why it is considered undesirable for parents to choose characteristics of their baby, such as eye colour.

....

....

b)   In what circumstances are parents allowed to choose the sex of their baby?

....

c)   What is the advantage of screening for genetic disorders?

....

d)   Some people object to embryos being screened for genetic disorders. Suggest why.

....

Stem Cells

Q1 **Stem cell research** is a potentially exciting but very **controversial** area of biology.

a) Explain what a stem cell is.

....

b) Give one place where stem cells can be found in the body of an adult.

....

c) Explain what the following statement means: *"Every cell was once a stem cell"*.

....

....

d) If a stem cell divides to form other cells, what type of division is this?

....

Q2 The graph shows estimated **spending** on **stem cell research** in the UK between 1980 and 2005.

a) Describe how spending on this type of research has changed over the period shown.

....

b) Suggest explanations for:

i) the low level of spending before 1990.

....

ii) the change between 2001 and 2002.

....

c) Stem cell research may eventually lead to new treatments for several different diseases. Parkinson's disease is one example. Name two other diseases that could be treated using stem cells, and explain how the stem cells might be used in each case.

1. ....

2. ....

Stem Cells

Q3 Some people are registered as **bone marrow donors**. Their bone marrow cells may be **transplanted** into a patient who needs them.

a) Name one disease that bone marrow transplants might be used for.

....

b) Bone marrow is a good source of **adult** stem cells, but stem cells from embryos are more useful from a medical point of view. Explain why.

....

....

Q4 Researchers were testing a new treatment. This involved injecting **embryonic stem cells** into the brains of patients with severe **Parkinson's disease**. After six months, the patients were tested to see if their symptoms had improved.

a) What symptoms would the patients with severe Parkinson's disease have shown?

....

b) If the treatment was successful, what would have happened to the stem cells inside the patients' brains?

....

c) Suggest a suitable control experiment that could be used in this investigation.

....

d) Give a possible ethical objection to this experiment, with regard to:

  i) the Parkinson's disease patients.

....

....

  ii) the source of the stem cells.

....

....

e) How do researchers try to control what type of cells are produced from stem cells?

....

Top Tips: Some of the countries that **don't** allow embryonic stem cell research **do** still allow abortions and IVF treatment, which pro-research types argue is a rather strange lack of consistency.

Mixed Questions — B3 Topic 1

Q1 Biochemists at the Gee-Fizz Drinks company use a **fungus** to synthesise **citric acid**.

a) Name a fungi that could be used in this process.

....

b) Explain why it's important to sterilise the container before the start of the process

....

....

c) What would you expect to happen to the pH of the container during fermentation? Explain your answer.

....

d) Gee-Fizz are currently developing low-calorie versions of their drinks. Explain how they could use enzymes to produce a drink with fewer calories.

....

....

e) Eating a lot of foods high in sugar and fat can lead to obesity. Fats are required in the diet but in moderation. Give two functions of fats in the body.

1. .... 2. ....

f) Jamie is obese, he claims that it is not because of his lifestyle. What else could have caused his obesity?

....

Q2 Mr and Mrs Milton have been trying to **conceive naturally** for the past three years but have so far been **unsuccessful**.

a) Give **three** reasons why they might not have been able to conceive naturally.

....

....

....

b) Treatments like IVF give couples like the Miltons the chance to be parents, however some people have ethical objections to IVF. Describe one ethical concern surrounding IVF.

....

....

14

Mixed Questions — B3 Topic 1

Q3 A company have developed a maize crop that is **frost resistant**. This allows maize to be grown in areas that have previously been to cold for the crop.

a) Describe how the frost-resistance gene is inserted into the maize.

....

....

....

b) Some people are opposed to the genetic modification of plants. Discuss the reasons why.

....

....

c) Modifying maize in this way is just one application of GM technology.
Describe how the following modifications to plants might be an advantage for humans.

   i) Leaves that contain insecticide.

   ....

   ii) Crops with increased nutritional value.

   ....

Q4 Geni-med is a company that is developing **new treatments** based on **genomics** (the study of organisms' genetic make-up).

a) Describe three potential medical applications of genomics.

....

....

....

....

b) Geni-med have identified a potential drug in a substance found in a plant.
Give two examples of drugs and the plants from which they have been obtained.

....

....

c) The company is also planning a number of experiments involving stem cells.
Explain how stem cells could be used to treat people with certain illnesses.

....

....

Instinctive and Learned Behaviour

Q1   Read the following passage and fill in the missing words.

genes	moisture	environment	learned	light	heat

Most behaviours seen in animals are due to both inherited and .... factors.

Inherited aspects of behaviour depend on the animal's ....

An example of inherited behaviour is the negative phototaxis of earthworms, where they move away from ....

Q2   Match up the aspects of **human behaviour** to show whether they are **instinctive** or **learned**.

Playing football

Salivating

Language

Sneezing

instinctive

learned

Q3   A student was studying the behaviour of **birds** on a **bird table**. Each day the student provided small pieces of cheese, some nuts hanging from the table on lengths of string, and some corn.

Below are some of the observations made by the student:

1. Robins took the cheese, but ignored the nuts and corn.

2. Pigeons took corn, but ignored the cheese. They expressed interest in the hanging nuts, but weren't able to get at them.

3. Great tits took some of the cheese, and managed to hang from the strings to take the nuts.

Occasionally a single crow visited the bird table. It initially took the cheese and corn, and watched the great tits. After the third week the student recorded that the crow took the nuts, they were able to get at them by hanging from the string.

a)   Give one example of a behaviour mentioned that seems to be **instinctive**, and explain your answer.

....

....

b)   Give one example of a behaviour mentioned that is **learned**, giving a reason for your answer.

....

....

c)   The student wanted to study how experiences in early life effect bird development. They kept a bird in isolation from a young age. What affect would you expect this to have on its song.

....

Top Tips: Animals are born with all the **nerve pathways** they need for **instinctive** behaviours **already connected**. The nerve pathways needed for **learned** behaviours develop with experience.

Instinctive and Learned Behaviour

Q4 An experiment was carried out into the **feeding behaviour** of **sea anemones**. Sea anemones are simple animals that live in marine rock pools, where they are found attached to rocks. Each has a ring of **tentacles** armed with stinging cells. Anemones use the stinging cells to paralyse smaller animals swimming in the water.

Two tanks of sea water each contained a single sea anemone. The behaviour of both the sea anemones was observed for **one hour**. A volume of 'fish extract' (made by crushing some dead fish in sea water) was placed in **one** of the tanks at a certain point within the hour of observation. The number of moving tentacles for each sea anemone was recorded at five minute intervals.

Time / minutes	No. of moving tentacles	
	Tank A	Tank B
0	2	2
5	1	1
10	10	2
15	7	0
20	4	2
30	3	0
40	4	0
50	4	1
60	4	2

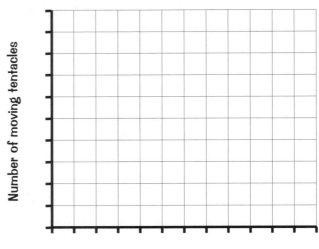

a) Draw graphs to illustrate the data on the grid provided. Use the same axes to show the results for both tanks.

b) Do you think the fish extract was added to tank A or to tank B? Explain your answer.

....

....

c) Suggest a time when the extract was added to the tank, giving a reason for your answer.

....

d) Suggest an explanation for what happened in the tank to which extract was added.

....

....

e) Do you think that this response is an example of learned or instinctive behaviour?

....

Q5 Explain what a '**Skinner box**' is and describe how it can be used to study animal behaviour.

....

....

....

Instinctive and Learned Behaviour

Q6 **Conditioning** is a type of **learned behaviour**.

  a) Explain the difference between '**classical** conditioning' and '**operant** conditioning'.

....

....

....

....

  b) Describe an example of:

    i) classical conditioning ....

    ii) operant conditioning ....

Q7 Identify each of the following examples of learned animal behaviour as either **classical conditioning** (**C**) or **operant conditioning** (**O**).

                                                            C   O

  a) A baby receives food, which makes it naturally happy. It only gets food when its mother is present. When its mother is present it feels happiness. ☐ ☐

  b) A rat is provided with a maze, at the end of which is a food reward. After many trials, the rat learns to complete the maze and reach the reward without error. ☐ ☐

  c) A child learns how to ride a bike. ☐ ☐

  d) A dolphin learns to associate being given food with its trainer blowing a whistle. ☐ ☐

Q8 **Habituation** is an important part of the learning process in young animals.

  a) Explain the term **habituation**.

....

....

  b) Explain why habituation is **beneficial** to animals.

....

Q9 **Guide dogs** for the blind undergo a period of intensive **training**. One part of this training involves teaching the dogs to stop at roadsides and wait for commands.

  a) Suggest one form of operant conditioning that could be used to ensure that the dog learns to stop at the roadside and wait for a command.

....

  b) Explain why operant conditioning involving rewards is preferable to operant conditioning involving punishments.

....

Social Behaviour and Communication

Q1 List three reasons why animals **communicate** with one another.

1. ....

2. ....

3. ....

Q2 Below is a list of different **types** of communication used by different kinds of animals. In each case, suggest a **reason** for the communication.

a) A female moth releases a pheromone into the air.

....

b) A butterfly flashes its wings to show spots that look like large, staring eyes.

....

c) A honey bee does a 'waggle dance' in the hive.

....

d) A dog rolls onto its back. ....

Q3 **Peafowl** are large birds related to pheasants. Male peafowl, called **peacocks**, have long coloured feathers that project beyond the tail. Peafowl live naturally in India, where they are sometimes preyed on by tigers.

a) Suggest a possible **advantage** of the long feathers of the peacock.

....

b) Suggest a possible **disadvantage** of having these long feathers.

....

c) Female peafowl, called peahens, are dull-coloured in comparison. Suggest why.

....

....

Q4 **Language** is the most obvious form of **human communication**, but there are others.

a) Give three methods of **non-verbal** communication between humans.

....

b) What is a possible advantage of verbal communication over non-verbal communication?

....

Social Behaviour and Communication

Q5 The **chiffchaff** and the **willow warbler** are two related species of woodland birds.
They are both green-brown in colour and spend much of their time among the foliage of trees.

a) Suggest why these birds attract mates using song rather than visual signals.

....

b) The song of the chiffchaff sounds very different from the song of a willow warbler.
Explain why this is necessary.

....

....

Q6 **Communication** can happen in many different ways.

a) Humans communicate using **speech** and birds communicate using **song**.
In what ways are these two forms of communication different?

....

....

b) Humans and many other mammals also use **facial expressions** to communicate.
Would you expect a **panda bear** to understand a human **frown**? Explain your answer.

....

Q7 When confronted with a **mirror**, a **dog** may look behind the mirror in an attempt to find
the 'other animal' presented to it. Suggest how this kind of reaction makes the behaviour
of the dog fundamentally **different** from the behaviour of a typical human being.

....

....

Q8 It's thought that humans are more **self-aware** than other animals.

a) Explain what is meant by the term **self-awareness**.

....

....

....

b) Explain why it is difficult to know whether other animals have 'self-awareness'.

....

Feeding Behaviours

Q1   Choose words from the list below to complete the following passage.

carnivores	vitamin A	herds	predators	amino acids	prey	herbivores	packs

Sheep, cows, horses and rabbits are ...., which means that they feed

on plant material. Many feed in groups called .... This makes it

more likely that at least a few individuals will be able to spot ....

A problem with a herbivorous diet is that it can be low in certain kinds of nutrients, such as

...., so herbivores have to spend a lot of time feeding.

Q2   The diagrams to the right show a **sheep skull** and a **cat skull**. Sheep are herbivores and cats are carnivores.

Sheep   Cat

a)   A sheep's eyes are on the **side** of its head, but a cat's eyes are at the **front**. Suggest why each species has evolved these features.

....

....

b)   Give one other difference between the skulls that could be related to different types of feeding.

....

....

Q3   **Wolves** work in packs when hunting large animals such as **reindeer**.

a)   Suggest why it is important for wolves to cooperate in this way when they hunt reindeer.

....

b)   Reindeer are usually found in **herds**. Give two reasons why this reduces the chances of any one particular reindeer being caught by a wolf pack.

....

....

....

c)   Explain why large herds of herbivores need to move around frequently.

....

d)   Wolves usually hunt **individually** for smaller prey such as rabbits. Suggest why.

....

B3 Topic 2 — Behaviour in Humans and Other Animals

Feeding Behaviours

Q4 Which of the following statements are most likely to apply to **herbivores**, and which to **carnivores**?

	herbivores	carnivores
a) They have strong horns for defence.	☐	☐
b) They eat food that is high in protein.	☐	☐
c) They can go for several days without feeding.	☐	☐
d) They form groups with others of the same species for safety.	☐	☐
e) They form groups with others of the same species to get food.	☐	☐

Q5 Read the following passage about the feeding behaviour of **spiders**.

> All spiders are predators. They have fangs connected to poison glands. When they bite prey with their fangs, they inject the poison which quickly paralyses the prey. Some spiders ambush their prey, either by leaping on them (in the case of jumping spiders), or running them down (as with wolf spiders). Many spiders have glands that produce silk, which they use to spin webs — the webs produced by money spiders and orb-web spiders are used to trap flying insects. Funnel-web spiders lay trip-lines for their prey, and lie in wait for them in holes in the ground.

a) Give two **structural** features of spiders that make them good predators.

....

b) The poison of many spiders works so quickly that the prey is paralysed almost immediately. Suggest why it is important that the poison works quickly.

....

c) Describe three ways in which different spiders catch their prey.

....

....

Q6 Some animals use **tools** to get food.

a) Give two examples of animals using tools.

1. ....

2. ....

b) Some species of vulture break open bones to reach the nutritious marrow inside by dropping the bones onto rocks. Would you class the rocks as tools in this case? Explain your answer.

....

....

Feeding Behaviours

Q7 Adult **birds** respond to **stimuli** from their young, which prompt them to supply **food**.

a) Describe the ways in which parent birds may be stimulated to feed their offspring.

....

....

b) Explain why both parent and young are using instinctive (inherited) behaviour when a bird feeds its offspring.

....

....

Q8 Experiments were carried out to investigate the '**begging response**' in young **herring gulls**. The young peck at the bill of the parent to stimulate it to regurgitate fish, which the young then swallow. This behaviour occurs soon after the young hatch. Scientists presented young herring gulls with a series of **cardboard models** of a parent gull's head. The results of the study are shown below. Real adult herring gulls have a **white head**, with a **yellow bill** and a **red spot** near the tip.

Model	White head, grey bill, no spot	White head, grey bill, red spot	White head, yellow bill, red spot	Pointed red stick with three white bands
No. of pecks by young	5	39	42	50

a) Describe what these experiments demonstrate about what stimulates the begging response in young herring gulls. Explain your answer.

....

....

....

b) Is the begging response instinctive or learned? Give a reason for your answer.

....

....

c) It's thought that parent birds are also stimulated to regurgitate food by the wide open, brightly coloured mouths of chicks begging for food. Describe how you could test whether it's the **colour** or the **size** of a chick's open mouth (or both) which stimulates the parent to regurgitate food.

....

....

Reproductive Behaviours

Q1 Draw lines to match up each animal below with the most likely way in which a **male** of that species would **attract a mate**.

mandrill monkey

display aggression to other males

red deer

mating call

frog

pheromone

moth

display brightly coloured parts of body

Q2 Explain what is meant by the following terms:

a) monogamy

....

b) harem

....

c) courtship

....

Q3 In many species of **birds**, **both** parents play a role in incubating eggs and feeding the young once the eggs have hatched.

a) State an advantage of this shared responsibility for:

i) the young. ....

....

ii) the parents. ....

....

b) **Birds of paradise** differ in that the females have sole responsibility for looking after the young. These birds live on the island of New Guinea, where there are few predators.

Suggest a possible link between the reproductive behaviour of birds of paradise and the fact that there are few predators in their habitat.

....

....

....

Reproductive Behaviours

Q4   In most species, **males compete** to win the right to mate with females. Methods used vary from bringing the female gifts of food to fighting off the other males. However, it is the **opposite** way around in **seahorses** — females compete for the attention of males. Seahorses are also unusual in that the female lays her eggs in the male's pouch and **he** is then '**pregnant**' with the young and eventually gives birth to them.

a)   Explain fully why males usually compete for females, and why this is not the case in seahorses.

....

....

....

....

....

b)   Why is it important for most animals that females don't mate with a male of a closely related species?

....

....

Q5   Some young birds and mammals develop a simple kind of behaviour early in their life called '**imprinting**', where learned behaviour becomes fixed and resistant to change. Ducklings, for example, develop imprinted behaviour when they **instinctively follow** the first thing they see move — which usually is their mother.

a)   The imprinting behaviour of ducklings is inherited and not learned.
Explain how you can tell this from the description above.

....

....

b)   Give one advantage of imprinting behaviour in ducklings.

....

....

c)   Suggest one part of a duckling's behaviour that will be learned, rather than inherited.

....

Top Tips: The male **bowerbird** impresses females by constructing an elaborate mound of earth decorated lavishly with shells, leaves, feathers and flowers, which he spends **hours** carefully arranging.

Reproductive Behaviours

Q6 Some animals **care for their young** for long periods, while others provide **no parental care** at all.

a) Name three animals that care for their young, and three that do not.

Care: ....

Don't care: ....

b) Give three ways in which animals may care for their young.

1. ....

2. ....

3. ....

Q7 Male **crickets** and **grasshoppers** attract females by a process called 'stridulation', where they rub rough parts of their body together. Crickets rubs their wings together and grasshoppers rub their legs over their wings. The result is a **chirping sound**.

a) Different species of crickets and grasshoppers produce different patterns of chirps, in terms of volume, pitch and frequency of chirps. Explain why.

....

....

b) The 'songs' of different species of grasshopper are more distinctive than the songs of different species of cricket. What does this suggest about the **appearance** of different species of the two kinds of insects. Explain your answer.

....

....

....

Q8 Parental care is a **successful evolutionary strategy**.

a) Explain why.

....

....

b) Why is a shorter pregnancy less risky to a mother than a long pregnancy?

....

....

Human Evolution and Development

Q1 Scientists think that humans are most **closely related** to a species of ape called a **bonobo**.

a) Explain how scientists know this.

....

b) Give one difference in behaviour between humans and bonobos.

....

Q2 Suggest how each of the following has contributed to the **success** of the **human species**:

a) Tool use.

....

....

b) Living in large, complex societies.

....

....

Q3 Below are some of the key events in the **evolution** of **human behaviour**.

> **2.5 million yrs ago** — earliest use of stone tools.
>
> **50 000 yrs ago** — hunter-gatherer society.
>
> **10 000 years ago** — farming begins in some parts of the world.

a) Explain what is meant by 'hunter-gatherer society'.

....

....

b) Explain how the use of tools would have been beneficial in such a society.

....

....

c) Suggest one advantage of a farming system over a hunter-gatherer system.

....

....

Human Evolution and Development

Q4   Humans have **domesticated** a range of animal species.

a)   Dogs were one of the first species to become domesticated.
Explain the advantage to the humans living at this time of domesticating dogs.

....

....

b)   Choose reasons from the list below for domesticating the following animals.

A For hide	B Farming the land	C For Food

D For travelling	E Carrying heavy loads	F For a table tennis partner

Horse: ....

Cattle: ....

c)   Give one example of how selective breeding has been used to modify the characteristics of a domesticated animal.

....

....

Q5   'Human' society has changed significantly in the last two million years.

a)   Give three main ways in which we currently modify our environment.

1. ....

2. ....

3. ....

b)   We use **tools** to modify our environment. Other animals, e.g. chimps, also use tools.
Suggest why humans rather than chimps have been able to develop farming and build cities.

....

....

Top Tips: Our ancestors used to swing through trees. Then they started to walk on two legs a bit. They gradually left the trees and, about two million years ago, began to use simple **tools** — and then it was just a short hop, skip and jump to games consoles and microwaves.

B3 Topic 2 — Behaviour in Humans and Other Animals

Human Behaviour Towards Animals

Q1 Name **one animal** that is used for each purpose given below.

a) Providing wool ....

b) Hunted for sport ....

c) Racing ....

Q2 Many different species of animal are kept in **zoos**. Some people think that this is **necessary**, but others think it is **cruel**. Outline the reasons for and against keeping animals in zoos.

....

....

....

....

Q3 Animals are often used to test **drugs** before they are released for human use.

a) Explain why many people think this is necessary.

....

b) Suggest one reason why some people feel it is cruel to use animals in this way.

....

They're looking for a bit more in these than 'because it's cruel'.

c) Give one other way in which laboratory animals could be of use in medicine.

....

Q4 Some people feel that animals should have the **same rights** as humans.

a) Animals are used for entertainment in some circuses.

i) Give one reason why some people might be against this.

....

ii) Explain how a circus owner might justify this use of the animals.

....

b) Animals are also bred for food. They are often intensively farmed. Explain:

i) why some people think that this is wrong.

....

ii) how this use of animals could be justified.

....

Mixed Questions — B3 Topic 2

Q1   Many people keep **dogs** either as **companions** or as **working** animals.
The domesticated dog is similar in many ways to **wild dogs** which live in parts of Africa.

a)   A domesticated dog can be taught to 'sit' by rewarding it every time it responds correctly to the
'sit' command. What type of conditioning is this an example of? Underline the correct answer.

classical   operant

b)   Many domesticated dogs are useful as guards, because they will bark loudly if they hear a burglar
breaking into the house, but don't bark at noises from people or cars just passing the house.

    i)   Explain why dogs respond to the quiet noise of a burglar but not to the louder noise from cars.

....

....

    ii)   Give two other examples of how dogs are useful to humans, apart from guarding property
and providing companionship.

....

c)   Both wild dogs and domesticated dogs feed their young on milk for several weeks after birth.
How does a newborn puppy 'know' to suckle from its mother?

....

d)   African wild dogs are carnivores. Their prey includes gazelles (shown
in the picture), which are herbivores. Gazelles spend much more time
eating than wild dogs do. Explain this difference.

....

....

e)   After birth, young wild dogs spend several months with their parents, who protect them from
predators and teach them to hunt effectively.

    i)   Outline the possible **disadvantages** for the parents of this behaviour.

....

    ii)   Explain why this behaviour is a **good evolutionary strategy**, despite its disadvantages.

....

....

Q2   **Swans** mate for life — once a pair have mated, they only breed with each other.
Explain why this behaviour is unusual, and describe some more common mating patterns.

....

....

Mixed Questions — B3 Topic 2

Q3 Wildebeest are a type of buffalo which graze on **short grass**. During the dry season they move from place to place in large **herds**. Wildebeest are commonly preyed on by **lions**.

a) Why do you think herds of wildebeest have to move frequently during the dry season?

....

b) Explain why it is advantageous for the wildebeest to move and graze in large herds.

....

....

Q4 **Humans** are closely related to **bonobos** (a kind of ape) and share many **behaviours** with them.

a) It's thought that humans first developed agriculture about 10 000 years ago. Before then, how did humans obtain food?

....

b) In every part of the world, humans **smile** as a way of communicating **pleasure**. Would you expect bonobos to show pleasure by smiling? Explain your answer.

....

c) Both humans and apes (like bonobos) can use tools, and communicate in a variety of ways. Describe three ways in which humans are thought to be very **different** from all other animals.

....

....

....

....

Q5 Most **birds** reproduce by laying a **small** clutch of eggs, and keeping them warm until they hatch into **chicks**. They then tend the chicks in the nest for several weeks.

a) **Frogs** lay **large** clumps of frogspawn in a pond and then leave — they don't tend the spawn or the tadpoles which hatch from it. Explain why frogs don't need to look after their young but birds do.

....

....

b) The 'cheeping' of a young bird stimulates its parent to feed it. Give three other 'uses' of bird calls.

....

....

Mixed Questions — B3 Topic 2

Q6 **Male frigate birds** have red sacs on their chests. During the mating season, males **display** by inflating this sac, as shown in the picture.

a) What advantage might the male frigate bird gain from this behaviour?

....

....

b) In most bird species the female is **duller** in appearance than the male. Explain why this is.

....

....

Q7 **Golden eagles** are large birds of prey. Their diet includes smaller birds like **grouse** and mammals like **rabbits**. They catch their prey by diving down quickly and plucking it from the ground.

a) Golden eagles hunt as individuals.

i) Some carnivores hunt in packs. What advantages can this give them?

....

ii) Suggest why golden eagles **don't** hunt in packs.

....

b) Golden eagles have eyes at the **front** of their heads. Explain how this is important in terms of their feeding behaviour.

....

....

c) Suggest features of the following animals which help them avoid being caught by a golden eagle:

i) rabbits ....

....

....

ii) grouse ....

....

....

C3 Topic 3 — Chemical Detection

Analysing Substances

Q1   Use the words to complete the passage.

method	only	quantitative	sample	qualitative	much

The first stage in any analysis is to choose the most suitable analytical

...method............ A ...qualitative............... method can be used if you

...only.................... want to find out what substances are present in a

...sample..................., but if you want to find out how ....much...................

of each substance is present then a ..quantitative.......... analysis is necessary.

Q2   Explain why it might be important to know:

a)   the concentration of **chlorine** in a swimming pool ...because chlorine is used to kill

bacteria in the water, if there is to not enough, it could be dangerou

b)   the concentration of **alcohol** in blood ...if there has been a crime committed

forensic scientists could use this information in court..............

c)   the **nitrate ion** concentration in drinking water - so you can check the..............

purity and find out if there are any dangerous chemicals...

Q3   Maria was asked to identify the **solute** present in a sample of water.
It was known to be a single ionic compound.

Step 1 — Maria took 5 cm³ of the water and added a small quantity of sodium hydroxide solution.
A **white precipitate** was formed that dissolved when more of the alkali was added. This told Maria
that the **aluminium ion** was present.

Step 2 — Maria took a further 25 cm³ of water and added some dilute hydrochloric acid followed by
an excess of barium chloride solution. A **white precipitate** was formed showing Maria that the
sulphate ion was present.

a)   Circle the correct answer for each of the following questions.

i)   What sort of analysis is carried out in Step 1 of the procedure?   (qualitative)/ quantitative

ii)   What sort of analysis is carried out in Step 2 of the procedure?   (qualitative)/ quantitative

b)   What must be the identity of the mystery solute? ...aluminium sulphate..............

Top Tips: Chemical analysis isn't just for forensic scientists — it's important in chemistry too.
Make sure you know what qualitative and quantitative analyses are, and be ready to explain how you'd
identify ionic compounds — remember you have to test for both the positive and the negative ion.

Tests for Positive Ions

Q1 Robert adds a solution of **sodium hydroxide** to a solution of **calcium chloride**. The formula of the calcium ion is Ca^{2+}.

a) What would Robert observe?

a white precipitate would have been formed

b) Write the balanced symbol equation for the reaction, including state symbols.

$CaCl_2(aq) + 2NaOH(aq) \rightarrow Ca(OH)_2(s) + 2NaCl(aq)$

c) Write the balanced **ionic equation** for this reaction, including state symbols.

$Ca^{2+}(aq) + 2OH^-(aq) \rightarrow Ca(OH)_2(s)$

Q2 Les had four samples of **metal compounds**. He tested each one by placing a small amount on the end of a wire and putting it into a Bunsen flame. He observed the **colour of flame** produced.

a) Draw lines to match each of Les's observations to the metal cation producing the coloured flame.

brick-red flame — Na^+
yellow/orange flame — Cu^{2+}
blue-green flame — K^+
lilac flame — Ca^{2+}

b) Les wants to make a firework which will explode in his local football team's colour, **lilac**. Which of the following compounds should he use? Circle your answer.

silver nitrate   sodium chloride   barium sulphate   (potassium nitrate)   calcium carbonate

Q3 Cilla adds a few drops of **NaOH** solution to solutions of different **metal compounds**.

a) Complete her table of results.

Metal Cation	Colour of Precipitate
Fe^{2+}	Sludy green
Cu^{2+}	blue
Fe^{3+}	reddish brown
Al^{3+}	white then colourless. No precipitate

b) Complete the balanced ionic equation for the reaction of iron(II) ions with hydroxide ions.

$Fe^{2+}(aq) + 2 OH^-(aq) \rightarrow Fe(OH)_2 (s)$

c) Write a balanced ionic equation for the reaction of **iron(III) ions** with hydroxide ions.

$Fe^{3+}(aq) + 3OH^-(aq) \rightarrow Fe(OH)_3(s)$

Don't forget state symbols.

d) Cilla adds a few drops of sodium hydroxide solution to **aluminium sulphate solution**. She continues adding sodium hydroxide to excess. What would she observe at each stage?

White at first. Then redissolves in excess NaOH to form a colourless solution

C3 Topic 3 — Chemical Detection

Tests for Positive Ions

Q4   Claire was given a solid sample of a mixture of two ionic compounds. She was told that they were thought to be **ammonium chloride** and **calcium chloride**.

a)   Describe, in detail, how she would test for the presence of the two **positive ions**.

   ....

   ....

   ....

b)   What would she **observe** at each stage?

   ....

   ....

c)   Write **ionic equations** for the reactions that identify the positive ions.

   ....

   ....

Q5   Select compounds from the box to match the following statements.

KCl	LiCl	$FeSO_4$	NH_4Cl	$FeCl_3$	$Al_2(SO_4)_3$
NaCl	$CuSO_4$	$CaCl_2$	$MgCl_2$	$BaCl_2$	

a)   This compound forms a blue precipitate with sodium hydroxide solution.   ....

b)   This compound forms a white precipitate with sodium hydroxide
that dissolves if excess sodium hydroxide is added.   ....

c)   This compound forms a green precipitate with sodium hydroxide solution.   ....

d)   This compound forms a reddish brown precipitate with sodium
hydroxide solution.   ....

e)   This compound reacts with sodium hydroxide to release a pungent gas.   ....

f)   This compound reacts with sodium hydroxide to form a white precipitate,
and it also gives a brick-red flame in a flame test.   ....

Top Tips: Right, this stuff needs to be learnt properly. Otherwise you'll be stuck in your exam staring at a question about the colour that some random solution goes when you add something you've never heard of before to it, and all you'll know is that ammonia smells of cat wee.

Tests for Negative Ions

Q1 Give the chemical formulae of the **negative ions** present in the following compounds.

  a) barium sulphate .... **b)** potassium iodide .... **c)** silver bromide ....

Q2 Choose from the words given to complete the passage below.

carbon dioxide	limewater	hydrochloric acid	sodium hydroxide	hydrogen

A test for the presence of carbonates in an unidentified substance involves reacting it with dilute

.... If carbonates are present then .... will be

formed. You can test for this by bubbling it through .... to see if it

becomes milky.

Q3 Answer the following questions on testing for **sulphate** and **sulphite** ions.

  a) Which two **chemicals** are used to test for sulphate ions?

  ....

  b) What would you **see** after adding these chemicals to a sulphate compound?

  ....

  c) **i)** What substance is used to test for sulphite ions? ....

  ii) Describe what you would see after adding this substance to a sulphite compound.

  ....

  ....

Q4 Deirdre wants to find out if a soluble compound contains **chloride**, **bromide** or **iodide** ions. Explain how she could do this.

  ....

  ....

  ....

Q5 Complete the following symbol equations for reactions involved in **tests for negative ions**.

  a) $Ag^+(aq) +$ .... $\rightarrow AgCl(s)$

  b) $2HCl(aq) + Na_2CO_3(s) \rightarrow 2NaCl(aq) +$ ....(l) + ...(g)

  c) .... + ... $\rightarrow BaSO_4(s)$

You're being a bit negative today, aren't you?

No...

C3 Topic 3 — Chemical Detection

36

Tests for Acids and Alkalis

Q1 Acids and alkalis can be tested for using indicators.

a) Complete the following statement about litmus indicator with the correct colours.

Acids turn .... litmus ...., and alkalis turn .... litmus ....

b) Which ions are always present in an acid? ....

c) How would you test for the presence of an acid other than using an indicator? Describe the result of this test if an acid is present.

....

....

....

d) Which ions are always present in an alkali? ....

e) Other than using an indicator, how would you test for the presence of an alkali? Describe the result of this test if an alkali is present.

....

....

....

Q2 Ammonia gas can be prepared in the laboratory by heating solid ammonium chloride with solid **calcium hydroxide**.

a) Write a balanced **symbol equation** for this preparation of ammonia.

....

b) Write the **ionic equation** for this reaction.

....

c) Describe how you could test for ammonia.

....

d) What colour will a solution of calcium hydroxide be with **phenolphthalein**?

....

Top Tips: Acids and alkalis is important stuff — and being able to explain how you'd identify H^+ and OH^- ions is a big indicator (ha ha) to the examiners of how much you know. So get learning...

C3 Topic 3 — Chemical Detection

Measuring Amounts — Moles

Q1 a) **Complete** the following sentence.

> One mole of atoms or molecules of any substance will have a .... in grams equal to the .... for that substance.

b) What is the **mass** of each of the following?

i) 1 mole of copper ....

ii) 3 moles of chlorine **gas** ....

iii) 2 moles of nitric acid (HNO_3) ....

iv) 0.5 moles of calcium carbonate ($CaCO_3$) ....

Q2 a) Write down the formula for calculating the **number of moles in a given mass**.

....

b) How many **moles** are there in each of the following?

i) 20 g of calcium ....

ii) 112 g of sulphur ....

iii) 200 g of copper oxide (CuO) ....

c) Calculate the **mass** of each of the following.

i) 2 moles of sodium ....

ii) 0.75 moles of magnesium oxide (MgO) ....

iii) 0.025 moles of lead chloride ($PbCl_2$) ....

Q3 Ali adds **13 g** of zinc to **50 cm³** of hydrochloric acid. All of the zinc reacts.

$$Zn + 2HCl \rightarrow ZnCl_2 + H_2$$

a) How many moles of **zinc** were added?

....

b) How many moles of **hydrochloric acid** reacted?

....

Measuring Amounts — Moles

Q4 Jenni added some **magnesium carbonate** to an excess of **dilute sulphuric acid**. A reaction occurred which produced 3 g of magnesium sulphate and some carbon dioxide gas.

a) Write a balanced **symbol equation** for the reaction.

....

b) What mass of **magnesium carbonate** did Jenni add to the acid?

....

....

c) What mass of **sulphuric acid** was used up in the reaction?

....

....

d) What mass of **carbon dioxide** was produced?

....

....

Q5 Dr Burette adds **0.6 g** of sodium to water. Sodium hydroxide and hydrogen form. (All the sodium reacts.)

a) Write a **balanced symbol equation** for this reaction.

....

b) What mass of **hydrogen** is produced?

....

....

c) Calculate the mass of **sodium hydroxide** produced.

....

....

Top Tips: So, you already know that the mole is not just a small burrowing animal. Now you need to make sure that you can convert between moles and grams. But that's not all — make sure you learn the formula for calculating the number of moles and you'll soon be sailing through those exam questions.

Calculating Volumes

Q1 Choose from the following words to complete the passage.

atmosphere	decreased	volume	26	higher
mass	increased	25	vole	mole	24

One .... of any gas will always occupy .... dm^3 when the

.... is measured at a temperature of .... °C and a pressure of

1 .... If the volume is measured at a .... temperature, the molar

volume of gas is increased. If the pressure is ...., the molar volume decreases.

Q2 The **limewater test** for carbon dioxide involves the reaction between carbon dioxide and calcium hydroxide, which is shown in the following equation:

$$CO_2 + Ca(OH)_2 \rightarrow CaCO_3 + H_2O$$

A solution of limewater containing 0.37 g of calcium hydroxide reacts with carbon dioxide at RTP.

a) What mass of **carbon dioxide** is needed to react completely with the limewater?

....

b) What **volume** does this amount of carbon dioxide occupy at RTP?

....

Q3 Methane burns in oxygen to produce carbon dioxide and water.

3.2 g of methane was completely burned in oxygen and the volume of each gas was measured. This was carried out at 112 °C and 1 atmosphere pressure. (1 mole of gas occupies 31 dm^3 at 112 °C and 1 atmosphere pressure.)

a) Write a balanced **equation** for the reaction.

....

b) What volume of **methane** was used in the reaction?

....

c) How much **oxygen** (in dm^3) reacted with the methane?

....

Don't forget that water is a gas at temperatures above 100 °C.

d) Calculate the **total volume of products** formed in this reaction.

....

....

Quantitative Chemistry and Solutions

Q1 Complete the table.

MOLES	VOLUME	CONCENTRATION (moles/dm³)
2	4 dm³	a)
0.5	2 dm³	b)
0.2	500 cm³	c)
0.2	100 cm³	d)

Q2 Work out how many **moles** of sodium hydroxide there are in:

a) 2 dm³ of a 0.5 M sodium hydroxide solution.

....

b) 100 cm³ of a 0.1 M sodium hydroxide solution.

....

Q3 Convert the solution concentrations below from **moles/dm³** to **g/dm³**.

a) 2 mol/dm³ sodium hydroxide, NaOH. ....

How many moles?

....

b) 0.1 mol/dm³ glucose, $C_6H_{12}O_6$. ....

....

Q4 Susan wants to work out the concentration of a solution of sodium chloride. She puts 5 ml of the solution in a pre-weighed, clean, dry evaporating basin and heats the basin until all the water appears to have evaporated.

a) What would Susan do next? Explain why she would do this.

....

....

b) After doing this, how can she calculate the mass of sodium chloride that was dissolved?

....

....

Q5 **10 cm³** of potassium chloride solution was heated gently to evaporate all the water. The mass of the basin and dry potassium chloride was **50.400 g**. (The mass of the basin when empty was 49.655 g.)

Calculate:

a) The **mass concentration** of the solution of potassium chloride.

....

b) The **molar concentration** of the solution of potassium chloride.

....

Titrations

Q1 Work out the number of **moles** in the following solutions.

a) 1 dm³ of 2 mol/dm³ HCl.

....

b) 100 cm³ of 1 mol/dm³ NaOH.

....

c) 25 cm³ of 0.1 mol/dm³ HNO_3.

....

d) 10 cm³ of 0.2 mol/dm³ $Ca(OH)_2$.

....

Q2 Circle the answer which best completes each of these sentences.

a) During acid/alkali titrations...

...methyl orange is always a suitable indicator.   ...the alkali must always go in the burette.

...the tap is opened fully near the end of the titration.   ...the flask is swirled regularly.

b) Phenolphthalein was added to sodium hydroxide in a flask as part of a titration with an acid. The indicator colour change at the end-point of the titration was...

...yellow/orange to red.   ...red to yellow/orange.

...colourless to pink.   ...pink to colourless.

Q3 A **titration** procedure was used to compare the **acid concentration** of some fizzy drinks. The acids present included carbonic, citric and ethanoic.

a) Name the **independent variable** and the **dependent variable** in this experiment.

Independent variable: ....

Dependent variable: ....

b) Suggest a suitable **indicator** and describe the **colour change** which would occur.

....

The titration values (titres) are shown in the table below.

fizzy drink	1st titre (cm³)	2nd titre (cm³)
Lemade	15.2	14.6
Kolafizz	20.5	19.8
Cherriade	12.6	12.1

c) Which drink contained the most acid?

....

Titrations

Q4 The concentration of some limewater, **Ca(OH)$_2$**, was determined by titration with hydrochloric acid, **HCl**. **50 cm³** of limewater required **20 cm³** of **0.1 mol/dm³** hydrochloric acid to neutralise it. Work out the concentration of the limewater in **g/dm³** using the steps outlined below.

a) How many moles of HCl are present in 20 cm³ of 0.1 mol/dm³ solution?

....

b) Complete the equation for the reaction.

.... + ... → CaCl$_2$ + ...

c) From the equation, ... mole(s) of HCl reacts with .... mole(s) of Ca(OH)$_2$.

d) Use your answers to a) and c) to work out how many moles of Ca(OH)$_2$ there are in 50 cm³ of limewater.

....

e) What is the concentration of the limewater in **moles per dm³**?

....

f) What is the concentration of the limewater in **grams per dm³**?

....

Q5 In a titration, **10 cm³** of sulphuric acid was used to neutralise **30 cm³** of **0.1 mol/dm³** potassium hydroxide solution.

$$H_2SO_4 + 2KOH \rightarrow K_2SO_4 + 2H_2O$$

a) What was the concentration of the sulphuric acid in **moles per dm³**?

....

....

....

....

....

b) What is the concentration of the sulphuric acid in **grams per dm³**?

....

....

Top Tips: Aargh, not calculations... As if Chemistry wasn't tricky enough without some maths getting involved too (but at least it's not as bad as Physics). Actually, these aren't the worst calculations — as long as you remember to tackle them in stages and you know your equations.

Water

Q1   Suggest two ways in which water is used in each of the following places.

a)   In the home ....

b)   In agriculture ....

c)   In industry ....

Q2   Indicate whether the following statements are true or false.

		True	False
a)	Water dissolves many ionic compounds.	☐	☐
b)	Water dissolves many covalent compounds.	☐	☐
c)	Sugars, salts and amino acids are transported around the body in solution in water.	☐	☐
d)	Many diseases, like cholera, are carried by microorganisms in water.	☐	☐

Q3   Answer the questions about water.

a)   Why is water called the **universal solvent**?

....

b)   How does water dissolve an **ionic** compound?

....

....

c)   Why is water essential for **life**?

....

....

d)   Why are many **power stations** situated next to rivers? ....

....

e)   Why is it important not to **waste** water?

....

....

Top Tips: Water has lots of everyday uses that we take for granted — make sure you can list some of these. You also need to know the importance of purifying water and not wasting it.

Water

Q4 Read the passage about water and answer the questions that follow.

> All sorts of substances get mixed with tap water. They include shampoo, toothpaste, washing powder and detergents, grease, body waste, sand and various waste from factories. All this goes down the plug hole into the drains and becomes known as sewage. The sewage flows through underground pipes to a sewage plant, where the water in it is cleaned up and put back into the river or water supply.
>
> The sewage is first pumped through a screen to remove any rags, paper and large debris. It goes into settling tanks where most of the solids sink to the bottom. Chemicals are then added to make all the smaller particles stick together. The clean water is taken off the top and put into the river. The sludge that remains is treated with special bacteria that break down the harmful compounds. The digested sludge is either put in landfill sites, burned to produce energy or put on the land as fertiliser. Not many years ago, all the sludge would have been dumped in the sea.

a) What activities in the **home** would put substances into sewage?

....

b) Why are chemicals added to the **settling tanks**?

....

c) Give one advantage and one disadvantage of **burning digested sludge**.

....

....

d) Give one advantage and one disadvantage of putting sludge in **landfill**.

....

....

Q5 Water needs to be very pure for **drinking** and for use in **power station boilers**.

a) Explain why water used in power stations boilers needs to be very pure.

....

....

b) Give **three** things that are carried out at water treatment works to make the water purer.

....

....

Mixed Questions — C3 Topic 3

Q1 Sam is taking part in a chemistry competition where she needs to be able to identify various **ions**.

a) Sam has a flowchart to help her identify **halide ions** present in a water sample. Complete the gaps in her flowchart.

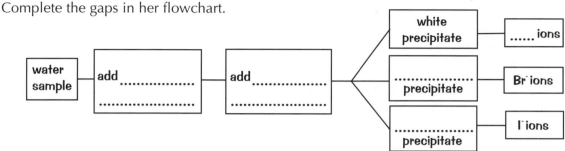

b) What type of analysis would this be? ....

c) Sam has another flowchart for identifying **positive ions**. Fill in the gaps.

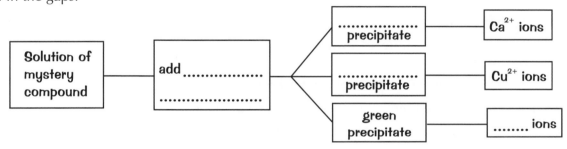

d) Sam knows that if she adds sodium hydroxide solution to a solution of aluminium ions, there will be a white precipitate which will then redissolve in excess sodium hydroxide to form a colourless solution. Write the ionic equations including state symbols for these two reactions.

....

....

e) Sam wants to test for H^+ ions in a solution. Describe how she could do this.

....

....

f) Describe how Sam could test for the presence of SO_3^{2-} ions in a substance.

....

....

g) Why will water dissolve many of the ionic compounds that Sam tests?

....

....

Mixed Questions — C3 Topic 3

Q2 Magnesium reacts with nitric acid, HNO_3, to form **magnesium nitrate**, $Mg(NO_3)_2$, and hydrogen.

a) Work out the relative formula mass of magnesium nitrate.

....

b) When 0.12 g of magnesium reacted with excess acid, 0.74 g of magnesium nitrate was formed.

    i) Calculate the number of moles of magnesium that reacted and the number of moles of magnesium nitrate produced.

    ....

    ....

    ii) The total volume of the solution formed was 0.2 dm^3. Work out the concentration of magnesium nitrate in this solution using your answer from part i).

    ....

    iii) If 0.025 moles of nitric acid was used, what mass of nitric acid was this?

    ....

    iv) Calculate the volume of hydrogen produced in the reaction (at RTP).

    ....

    ....

    ....

Q3 Jim carried out a **titration** as part of his chemistry coursework.

a) In his titration, Jim used 20 cm^3 of sulphuric acid to neutralise 35 cm^3 of 0.1 M sodium hydroxide solution. Find the concentration of the acid.

....

....

....

....

b) Suggest an indicator which Jim could have used during his titration, and give the colours it would be in acidic and alkaline solutions.

Indicator: ....

Acidic solution: ....

Alkaline solution: ....

Transition Elements

Q1   Complete the passage below by circling the correct word(s) from each pair.

> Most metals are in the transition block found **at the left** / **in the middle** of the periodic table.
>
> The transition metals are usually **reactive** / **unreactive** with oxygen and water. They generally
>
> have high **densities** / **volatilities** and **low** / **high** melting points. They are **good** / **poor**
>
> conductors of heat and electricity. Their compounds are often **coloured** / **shiny** and, like the
>
> metals themselves, are effective **fuels** / **catalysts** in many reactions.

Q2   Circle the correct answer for each of the following questions.

a)   Which one of the following properties applies to **all metals**?

  high density   good conductivity   high tensile strength

b)   Which one of the following properties applies to **all transition metals**?

  high melting point   poor conductivity   colourful

c)   Which property of most transition metals makes them useful as **pigments** and **dyes**?

  colourful compounds   high melting point   shiny appearance

Q3   Transition metals and their compounds often make **good catalysts**.

Draw lines to match the metals and compounds below to the reactions they catalyse.

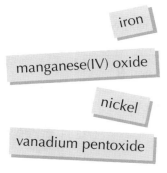

iron

manganese(IV) oxide

nickel

vanadium pentoxide

converting natural oils into fats

ammonia production

decomposition of hydrogen peroxide

sulphuric acid production

Q4   'Chemical gardens' can be made by sprinkling **transition metal salts** into **sodium silicate solution**. Transition metal silicate crystals grow upwards as shown.

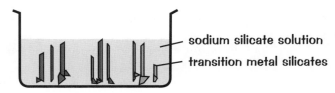

sodium silicate solution

transition metal silicates

Circle the three colours that you would be likely to see in the garden if potassium chromate(VI), potassium manganate(VII) and copper(II) sulphate crystals are used.

  red   orange   yellow   green   blue   purple

Transition Elements

Q5   Draw lines to connect the correct phrases in each column.
One has been done for you.

Metal / Alloy	Other Elements	Use
low-carbon steel	nothing	blades for tools
iron from a blast furnace	chromium	cutlery
high-carbon steel	0.1% carbon	car bodies
stainless steel	1.5% carbon	ornamental railings

Q6   Copper is commonly used in **electrical wires** and **plumbing**.

a)   Give three properties of copper that are **typical** of transition elements.

....

b)   Give another property that makes it ideal for use in:

i) electrical wiring ....

ii) plumbing ....

Q7   Read the description of **metal X** and answer the question that follows.

> **Metal X is found in the block of elements between Group 2 and 3 of the periodic table. It has a melting point of 1860 °C and a density of 7.2 g/cm³. The metal is used to provide the attractive coating on most motorbikes and bathroom taps. The metal forms two coloured chlorides, XCl₂ (blue) and XCl₃ (green).**

Identify five pieces of evidence in the passage which suggest that metal X is a transition metal.

1. ....

2. ....

3. ....

4. ....

5. ....

Alcohols

Q1 Alcohols are a common group of chemicals.

a) What is the general formula of an alcohol? ....

b) Complete the following table.

Alcohol	No. of Carbon Atoms	Molecular Formula	Displayed Formula
Methanol			
	2		
		C_3H_7OH	
			H H H H | | | | H–C–C–C–C–O–H | | | | H H H H
	5		

Q2 The molecular formula for **ethanol** can be written as C_2H_5OH or as C_2H_6O.

a) What is the functional group found in all alcohols? ....

b) Explain why it is better to write ethanol's formula as C_2H_5OH.

....

Q3 Complete the following passage using the words below.

fuel	diesel	non-renewable	fermentation	lubricant	land
more	renewable	oxidation	sunshine	petrol	less

Ethanol can be mixed with .... and used as a .... for

cars. The more ethanol used in the mixture, the .... pollution

produced. In some countries ethanol is made by the .... of plants

such as sugar cane. Making ethanol this way uses a natural and ....

resource. The sugar cane can be grown continuously, but you need plenty of

.... and ....

Alcohols

Q4 Tick the correct boxes to show whether the following statements are **true** or **false**. **True False**

a) Ethanol is a clear, colourless liquid at room temperature. ☐ ☐

b) Methanol is a non-volatile alcohol. ☐ ☐

c) Propanol is miscible with water. ☐ ☐

d) Alcohols burn to produce sulphur dioxide and water. ☐ ☐

e) Alcohols can react with oxygen to produce carboxylic acids. ☐ ☐

f) Alcohols can react with carboxylic acids to produce alkanes. ☐ ☐

g) Methanol is less toxic than ethanol. ☐ ☐

Q5 **Ethanol** is commonly used as a **solvent**.

a) Which part of ethanol's structure allows it to dissolve substances like hydrocarbons, oils and fats?

....

b) Which part of ethanol's structure allows it to mix with water and dissolve ionic compounds?

....

c) Ethanol is used in such things as glues, varnishes, printing inks, paints, deodorants and aftershaves. Give **two** properties of ethanol that often make it a good choice as a solvent.

....

Hint — these products need to 'dry'.

d) **Meths** is ethanol with other chemicals added to it. Give two of the other chemicals and explain why they're added.

1. ....

2. ....

Q6 Name the alcohol described in the passage below.

When alcohols react with oxygen they don't lose any of their carbon atoms.

> The alcohol is a clear colourless liquid that is **volatile**. It is completely **miscible** with water. When it reacts with oxygen it produces a carboxylic acid with **3 carbon atoms**.

Alcohol = ...

> **Top Tips:** You need to know the **structures**, **formulae**, **physical properties** and the **uses** of alcohols. And I don't just mean in the production of alcoholic drinks. There are lots of other potentially far more useful things you can do with alcohol — like using it as a fuel in cars (but I wouldn't suggest tipping your dad's favourite whisky into his car — he probably won't be best pleased).

Carboxylic Acids

Q1 Tick the correct boxes to show whether the following statements are **true** or **false**.

	True	False
a) Carboxylic acids have the functional group –COOH.	☐	☐
b) There are six carbon atoms in every molecule of propanoic acid.	☐	☐
c) The longer the hydrocarbon chain, the less soluble a carboxylic acid is in water.	☐	☐
d) Ethanoic acid reacts with sodium hydroxide to produce sodium ethanoate and water.	☐	☐

Q2 Match up the following carboxylic acids to the correct statement.

Methanoic acid...

Citric acid...

Ethanoic acid...

Butanoic acid...

...has four carbon atoms in every molecule.

...is produced when beer is left in the open air.

...has the displayed formula $H-C{\overset{=O}{\underset{O-H}{}}}$

...is used as a descaler.

Q3 Use the words given to complete the passage about everyday **carboxylic acids**.

fatty	regular	detergents	aspirin	blood	preservative	cheese
attacks	chubby	rayon	relief	nylon	oranges	vinegar

Carboxylic acids are an important part of several substances used in the home. Ethanoic acid is found in ...., which is not only used as a .... and flavouring, but is also used in the manufacture of the clothing fibre, ... Citric acid is present in fruits like .... and lemons and is used in fizzy drinks. .... is widely used for pain .... and has been shown to reduce .... clotting. Many people at risk of heart .... take aspirin on a .... basis. Longer chain carboxylic acids are commonly called .... acids and are used in ....

Q4 **Ethanoic acid** reacts with **calcium** like any other acid would.

a) Write the word equation for this reaction.

....

b) Write the balanced symbol equation for this reaction.

....

c) Suggest two safety precautions that should be taken when handling carboxylic acids.

....

Esters

Q1   Complete the sentences below by circling the correct word from each pair.

a)   The fruit flavours used in some sweets are made by mixing man-made **esters / alcohols** together.

b)   Esters **do / don't** mix very well with water, and **do / don't** mix well with alcohols.

c)   Most esters are colourless **gases / liquids**.

d)   Esters **are / aren't** volatile.

e)   Many esters are highly **unreactive / flammable**, which can lead to a flash **fire / flood**.

Q2   Name the **ester** formed from the following combinations of **alcohols** and **carboxylic acids**.

a)   ethanol + methanoic acid   ....

b)   methanol + propanoic acid   ....

c)   propanol + ethanoic acid   ....

Ha ha ha - snort - ha ha ha haaa! You're giving me esterics!

Q3   **Methanol** reacts with **propanoic acid** to produce **methyl propanoate** and water.

a)   Draw the displayed formula equation for this reaction in the space below.

b)   Name a catalyst that can be used in this reaction.   ....

c)   What type of reaction is this?   ....

Q4   Esters are commonly used in **perfumes**, **flavourings** and as **solvents**.

a)   i)   Why are esters used in perfumes? ....

     ii)   Why isn't it a good idea to take a deep breath when smelling esters?

       ....

b)   Suggest why some people worry about esters being used as food flavourings.

     ....

c)   i)   Why are esters used as solvents? ....

     ii)   Suggest why esters have replaced other organic solvents in things like paint.

       ....

Electrolysis

Q1 **Complete** and **balance** the following electrode reactions.
For each one, tick the correct box to show whether it is **oxidation** or **reduction**.

Oxidation   Reduction

a) ....$Cl^- \rightarrow Cl_2 + $........$e^-$ ☐ ☐

b) $Ni^{2+} + $........$e^- \rightarrow$ .... ☐ ☐

c) ....$O^{2-} \rightarrow O_2 + $........$e^-$ ☐ ☐

d) ....$OH^- \rightarrow $........$H_2O + O_2 + $........$e^-$ ☐ ☐

e) $Al^{3+} + $............ $\rightarrow Al$ ☐ ☐

Q2 Electroplating could be used to put a thin coat of **silver** onto a **nickel** fork.

a) Complete the diagram by labelling the **cathode** and **anode**.

b) What ion must the electrolyte contain?

....

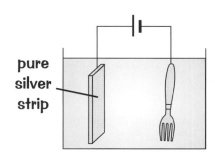

pure
silver
strip

Q3 **Molten copper(II) chloride** is electrolysed using carbon electrodes.

a) Write the half-equation for the reaction at the **anode**. ....

b) Write the half-equation for the reaction at the **cathode**. ....

c) Write the full **ionic equation** for the electrolysis of copper(II) chloride.

....

....

Q4 Study the reactivity series and the table showing the products at the cathodes when different solutions of **ionic compounds** are electrolysed.

What do you notice about the substance released at the cathode and where it's found in the reactivity series?

....

....

....

....

Ionic Compound Solution	Product at Cathode
sodium nitrate	hydrogen
copper sulphate	copper
sodium iodide	hydrogen
potassium chloride	hydrogen
silver nitrate	silver

reactivity ↑

potassium
sodium
calcium
carbon
zinc
iron
lead
hydrogen
copper
silver

Electrolysis and Cells

Q1 Tick the correct boxes to show whether the following statements are **true** or **false**.

True False

a) Copper is extracted from its ore by electrolysis. ☐ ☐

b) Copper needs to be very pure for use in electrical conductors. ☐ ☐

c) Batteries are electrochemical cells used to produce electricity. ☐ ☐

d) In electrolysis, electricity causes a chemical change. ☐ ☐

Q2 Copper is **purified** by electrolysis.

a) Draw a labelled diagram in the box provided to show the electrolysis cell used in the purification of copper.

b) Write half-equations for the reactions at each electrode.

Cathode: ....

Anode: ....

c) Explain why pure copper ends up at the **cathode**.

....

....

Q3 The diagram shows an **electrochemical cell**. Zinc is **more reactive** than iron.

a) i) Describe what is happening at the zinc strip.

....

....

....

ii) Write a half-equation for this reaction. ....

b) i) Bubbles of gas are produced on the iron strip, but the iron strip does not change in appearance or mass. Describe what is happening here.

....

....

ii) Write a half-equation for this reaction. ....

c) Describe how this cell produces an electric current.

....

....

The Alkali Metals

Q1   Join the different **sodium compounds** to their **uses**.

bleach

purification of aluminium ore

soaps and detergents

making ceramics

sodium carbonate

sodium hydroxide

making glass

paper manufacture

fibres

soda crystals

Q2   Complete the passage by choosing from the words below.

| molten | Li_2CO_3 | alkali | limewater | 3500 |
| transition | limestone | Na_2CO_3 | coloured | solid | 1500 |

To make glass, a mixture containing sand (SiO_2), sodium carbonate (.............................)

and .... ($CaCO_3$) is heated to .... °C. At this stage,

.... metal compounds can be added to the .... glass to

make it .... As it cools down, the glass turns ....

Q3   Susan's teacher put a piece of **potassium** into a beaker of water containing **universal indicator**.

a)   Describe what Susan should expect to see. ....

....

b)   Write a balanced symbol equation for the reaction, including state symbols.

....

Q4   The table shows the **melting points** of some Group I metals.

a)   What is unusual about the melting points of these metals?

....

b)   Describe the trend in the melting point as you move down this group.

....

Element	MELTING PT (°C)
Li	181
Na	98
K	63
Rb	39
Cs	28

c)   Complete the following sentences which describe other trends seen in the Group I elements:

i)   As you move down Group I, the **size** of the atoms ....

ii)   As you move down Group I, the alkali metals become .... to cut.

iii)   As you move down Group I, the **reactivity** ....

Sulphuric Acid

Q1 The Contact process is used to manufacture sulphuric acid.
Complete the table to show the **conditions** used in the Contact process.

Temperature:	
Pressure:	
Catalyst:	

Q2 **Complete** and **balance** the following equations involved in the Contact process.

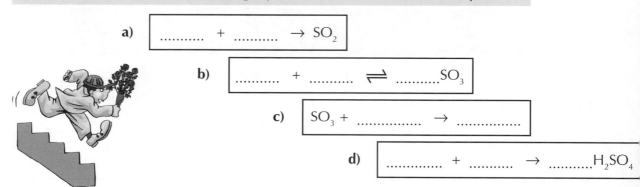

a) .... + ... → SO_2

b) .... + ... ⇌ ....SO_3

c) SO_3 + ... → ....

d) .... + ... → ....H_2SO_4

Q3 The graph shows the effect of **temperature** on the production of **sulphur trioxide**.

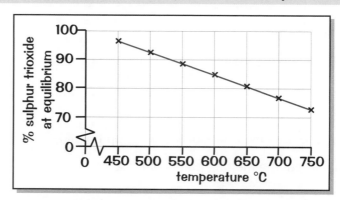

a) Describe how the percentage of sulphur trioxide at equilibrium changes with temperature.

....

b) At what temperature would you get 85% sulphur trioxide at equilibrium? ....

c) What percentage of sulphur trioxide would you get at equilibrium at 750 °C? ....

d) Explain why it is important to keep the pressure constant when investigating the effect of
temperature on percentage yield.

....

Sulphuric Acid

Q4   Complete the following sentences by circling the correct word from each pair.

> The **reduction** / **oxidation** of sulphur dioxide to sulphur trioxide is **exothermic** / **endothermic**.
>
> When the temperature is increased, you get **more** / **less** sulphur trioxide.
>
> If the temperature of any reaction is increased, the rate of the reaction **decreases** / **increases** because the particles have **more** / **less** energy.
>
> A high temperature gives a **high** / **low** yield of sulphur dioxide, but produces it **slowly** / **quickly**.

Q5   Modern industry uses thousands of tonnes of **sulphuric acid** per day.

a)   The pie chart shows the major uses of sulphuric acid. What is the **main use** of sulphuric acid?

....

Fibres 9%
Detergents 11%
Paints and Pigments 15%
Other Chemicals 16%
Fertilisers 32%
Other Uses 17%

b)   Give two uses of sulphuric acid in the car manufacturing industry.

1. ....

2. ....

c)   Which of the following compounds found in fertilisers is manufactured from sulphuric acid?

ammonium nitrate   ammonium sulphate   ammonium phosphate   potassium nitrate

d)   Describe how sulphuric acid is used in the preparation of metal surfaces.

....

....

Q6   As part of the Contact process, SO_2 is oxidised to form SO_3 at a pressure of **1-2 atmospheres**.

a)   Explain what would happen to the yield of SO_3 if the pressure was increased.

....

....

b)   Give two reasons why this oxidation is not done at a high pressure.

1. ....

2. ....

Top Tips: Concentrated sulphuric acid causes severe burns. So workers using it in all those industries in Q5 (it's really **economically important**) have to be very careful when handling it.

C3 Topic 4 — Chemistry Working for Us

Detergents

Q1   Many modern detergents used for washing clothes are 'biological'.

a)   What is the difference between biological and non-biological detergents?

....

b)   Why do biological detergents become less effective at temperatures above 40 °C?

....

c)   Circle the types of stain below that biological detergents would clean particularly effectively.

paint   blood   grass   tomato ketchup   engine oil

Q2   Fill in the blanks using the appropriate words below.

lowering	miscible	hydrophobic	immiscible
hydrophilic	lift	grease	sugar	raising

Oil and ....-based stains are .... with water. Surfactants help them to mix with water, by attaching to the fat molecules in the stain and by .... the surface tension of the water. The movement of the water in the washing machine helps the surfactant molecules to .... away droplets of oil into the water.

Q3   The diagram shows a **surfactant molecule**.

a)   Complete the diagram by labelling the **hydrophilic** and **hydrophobic** sections of the molecule.

....

b)   Which section of the molecule is attracted to:

i)   water molecules? .... ii)   grease and oil? ....

Q4   Surfactants are made when **fatty acids** react with **alkalis**.

a)   Complete the following general equation.   **acid** + **alkali** → .... + ...

b)   Suggest a suitable alkali to react with fatty acids to make soap. ....

c)   What name is given to this neutralisation reaction? ....

Detergents

Q5 Felicity works for a chemical company that is developing a new washing powder. She tests five different powders and records their cleaning effectiveness at different temperatures and against a range of different stains. She uses a scale of 1 (poor) to 10 (excellent).

a) Which powder is best at cleaning grass stains at 40 °C?

....

b) Which powders could be biological detergents? Give a reason for your answer.

....

....

....

		Washing powder				
		A	B	C	D	E
Effectiveness	at 40 °C	9	3	5	7	7
	at 60 °C	3	3	9	8	4
	Against tomato stains (at 40 °C)	8	1	5	4	10
	Against grass stains (at 40 °C)	8	4	5	7	3

Q6 In an experiment to investigate the **causes** of **hardness** in water, soap solution was added to different solutions. 'Five-drop portions' were added until a sustainable lather was formed.

Solution	Drops of soap solution needed to produce a lather	Observations on adding soap solution	Drops of detergent solution needed to produce a lather
distilled water	5	no scum	5
magnesium sulfate solution	35	scum formed	5
calcium chloride solution	30	scum formed	5
sodium chloride solution	5	no scum	5

a) i) Which ions caused hardness in the water?

....

ii) Explain how you know. ....

....

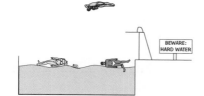

b) What role did the test using distilled water play in the experiment?

....

c) Suggest two advantages of using detergent solution rather than soap for washing.

....

d) Explain why scum forms when soaps are added to hard water.

....

e) Explain why water softeners are added to modern detergents.

....

Chemistry in Real Life

Q1 Use the information in the table to choose the **best** metal for the following applications. In each case explain why you think the metal is the best for that application.

Metal	Electrical Conductivity	Thermal Conductivity	Tensile Strength	Reaction with Water	Density (g/cm³)	Relative Cost
Steel	good	good	excellent	slow	7.8	cheap
Copper	excellent	excellent	good	none	9.0	very expensive
Aluminium	very good	very good	very good	none	2.7	expensive

a) The wires in electric cables. ....

b) Girders for building bridges. ....

c) Plating for the bottom of high-quality saucepans. ....

d) Lightweight parts for aircraft. ....

Q2 Isobel is developing a new range of **paints** and has asked for advice about the best chemicals to use. Her **product specification** is shown opposite.

- range of different colours
- they must be able to paint different materials (such as wood, paper and metals)
- they must not cost too much to make
- they must be safe to use
- they must dry quickly after being applied

a) Which group of elements are the coloured compounds in the paints likely to contain?

....

b) Suggest three important properties that the company will need to look at when assessing the suitability of different coloured compounds.

....

....

c) Two possible solvents for the paints are **water** and **ethanol**. Suggest two advantages and two disadvantages of using ethanol instead of water.

Advantages: ....

....

Think about how well each solvent matches up with the product specification.

Disadvantages: ....

....

___

Top Tips: Finally, some real-life examples where your expert knowledge might come in handy. Have a flick back if you need some reminders about the chemicals you've come across.

Mixed Questions — C3 Topic 4

Q1 An electronics company is investigating metals to make the 'legs' for a new type of **computer chip**. The 'legs' carry **electrical signals** in and out of the chips, as well as **holding** the chip in place. One possible metal for this job is **copper**.

a) Name **four** properties the metal should have.

....

....

b) **Copper** can be extracted from its ore by reduction with carbon.
Suggest why copper produced in this way could not be used for making the legs.

....

....

c) During the purification of copper by electrolysis, what is used as the:

i) cathode? ....

ii) electrolyte? ....

Q2 A new **perfume**, 'Back2Basics', is being released. The main ingredients are **water**, **alcohol** and a sweet smelling **ester**.

a) Give **two** properties of esters that make them well suited for use in perfumes.

....

b) Explain why the alcohol is present.

....

c) Another industrial use of alcohol is as a fuel. Give **two** advantages of using alcohol as a fuel.

....

Q3 Iron is a typical **transition metal**.

a) How is iron used in the Haber process for the production of ammonia?

....

b) Iron is alloyed with another element to form steel.

i) Name the other element in steel.

....

ii) Suggest one reason why iron is used as a structural material.

....

Mixed Questions — C3 Topic 4

Q4 Durden's Soap Company make soaps by reacting **esters** with **sodium hydroxide**.

a) The first stage in the process is to produce the ester.
Draw the displayed formula equation for the reaction between propanoic acid and ethanol.

b) During the production process workers in the factory are required to wear masks. Why is this?

....

c) Sodium hydroxide can be produced by reacting sodium with water.

i) Write a balanced symbol equation for the reaction between sodium and water.

....

ii) Sodium is an alkali metal. How does the reactivity of the alkali metals change as you move down the group?

....

iii) Give two properties that make alkali metals unlike other metals.

....

d) Durden's Soap Company also produce a range of detergents. Recently the company has received complaints about scum formation from people who live in hard water areas.

i) Why does this problem occur?

....

....

ii) What could the company add to their detergents to reduce this problem?

....

Q5 During the Contact process, **sulphur dioxide** reacts with **oxygen** to form **sulphur trioxide**.

a) Write the balanced symbol equation for this reaction.

....

b) **i)** What are the industrial conditions used during the production of sulphur trioxide?

....

ii) Why are these conditions a compromise? ....

....

Kinetic Theory and Temperature in Gases

Q1   Complete the following paragraph by choosing words from the box below.

0 °C	ice	0 K	100 °C	−273 °C	absolute	water

The Celsius temperature scale has two fixed points. One is the melting point of ....

at .... The other is the boiling point of .... at ....

The lowest fixed point on the kelvin temperature scale is at the lowest temperature possible

— called .... zero. This is given a value of .... and it is

equivalent to a temperature on the Celsius scale of about ....

Q2   Complete the following sentences by choosing the correct word from each pair.

a)   At 0 **°C / K** the internal energy of any substance is at its lowest possible value.

b)   When a gas is heated, the particles in it move **faster / more slowly**.

c)   The average **kinetic / potential** energy of particles in a gas is **equal / proportional** to the temperature
of the gas on the kelvin scale.

Q3   Convert the following temperatures to **kelvin** (K).

a)   3 °C   ....   **b)**   210 °C   ....

c)   −45 °C   ....   **d)**   0 °C   ....

Q4   Convert the following temperatures to **°C**.

a)   0 K   ....   **b)**   300 K   ....

c)   640 K   ....   **d)**   30 K   ....

Q5   The kinetic energy of particles depends on their mass and their velocity.

a)   What is the **formula** for the kinetic energy of a particle of mass **m** travelling at velocity **v**?

....

b)   The temperature of a gas is increased from 277 °C to 827 °C. At 277 °C the
mean kinetic energy of the gas is 1.14×10^{20} joules. What is it at 827 °C?

Always start a kinetic theory question involving temperature by converting degrees celsius to kelvin.

....

....

c)   Explain why it takes longer for the smell of air freshener to
spread through a room on a cold day than on a hot day.

....

64

Kinetic Theory and Pressure in Gases

Q1   **Kinetic theory** can be used to explain the behaviour and properties of gases.

a)   What does kinetic theory say that a gas consists of? Choose **two** options from A to E below.

   A stationary particles   B very small particles   C a rigid mesh of particles

   D mostly empty space   E fluctuations in electric and magnetic fields

b)   Explain how the impact of gas molecules on the sides of a container relates to the pressure of a gas

   ....

   ....

Q2   The apparatus shown in the diagram can be used to show how **pressure** changes with **temperature** for a gas.

a)   What variable is kept constant by having the gas in a rigid sealed container? Circle the correct letter.

   A Pressure   B Volume   C Temperature

b)   On the graph below, point A shows the pressure and temperature of the gas when an experiment began. Point B is the point at which the gas could not be heated any more with this apparatus. Explain why B occurs at a temperature of 100 °C.

   ....

   ....

c)   On the graph, continue the line to show how an ideal gas would behave if it was **cooled** to absolute zero.

d)   At what temperature in degrees celsius would the pressure be **zero**?

   ....

Q3   A bubble of carbon dioxide leaves a plant at the bottom of a lake. Initially it has a volume of **5 cm³** and is at a pressure of **6 atm**. The temperature at the bottom of the lake is **4 °C**. The bubble rises and just before it reaches the surface it is at a pressure of **1 atm** and a temperature of **20 °C**.

a)   Give two reasons why the volume of the bubble will **increase** as it rises.

   1. ....

   2. ....

b)   Calculate the **volume** of the bubble just before it reaches the surface.

   Don't forget to convert temperatures to kelvin.

   ....

   ....

Particles in Atoms

Q1 Alpha, beta and gamma are all types of ionising radiation, but they have quite different properties.

a) Rate the different types of radiation according to their penetrating power.

> 1 = high penetrating power
> 2 = moderate penetrating power
> 3 = low penetrating power

alpha ☐   gamma ☐

beta ☐

b) How does the **penetrating power** of each type of radiation compare to its **ionising power**?

....

c) Give an example of a material that can stop

 i) alpha radiation ....   **ii) beta** radiation ....

Q2 Complete the following sentences about **radioactive decay**.

a) During α decay, the nucleus loses .... protons and .... neutrons. So its mass number decreases by .... and its atomic number decreases by ....

b) During β^- decay a .... becomes a .... The atomic number increases by 1 and the mass number ....

c) During β^+ decay a .... becomes a .... The atomic number .... and the mass number stays the same.

d) α, β^+ or β^- decay results in the formation of a different ...., which is shown by the change in .... number.

e) When a nucleus emits a γ ray, its mass number changes by .... and its atomic number changes by ....

Q3 Neutrons are found in the nuclei of atoms and can also be emitted as a form of radiation. Underline the correct words from the options given.

a) Neutron radiation is **more / less** penetrating than alpha or beta radiation.

b) Neutrons do not have electric **charge / power** so they do not directly **absorb / ionise** material they pass through.

c) Absorbing a neutron can make a nucleus **ionised / radioactive**.

Particles in Atoms

Q4 The equation shows an isotope of carbon undergoing radioactive decay.

a) What type of radioactive decay is this?

....

$$^{14}_{6}C \longrightarrow X + ^{0}_{+1}e$$

b) Give the **nucleon number** and **atomic number** of element X.

nucleon number: .... atomic number: ....

c) People take precautions against cell damage from ionisation by most types of radiation. Why is it not necessary to take particular precautions against this type of radiation?

....

Q5 The graph on the right shows the number of neutrons (N) against the number of protons (Z) for **stable isotopes**.

a) What are **isotopes** of an element?

....

....

b) Are isotopes in region A stable or unstable? Circle your answer.

   stable   unstable

c) Are isotopes in region A neutron-rich or proton-rich?

   neutron-rich   proton-rich

d) Suggest a reason why isotopes in region B are **unstable**.

....

e) In order to achieve stability, what type of decay will isotopes in **region B** undergo?

....

f) What type of decay will isotopes in **region C** undergo in order to achieve stability?

....

g) What type of particle will isotopes in **region D** emit in order to become more stable?

....

Particles in Atoms

Q6   **Alpha particles** are strongly ionising.

a)   What kinds of atom undergo alpha decay?

....

b)   Circle the two of these elements that undergo alpha decay.   **H   U   Th   C   He**

c)   Complete this nuclear equation.

$$^{224}_{88}Ra \longrightarrow \boxed{}Rn \; + \; \boxed{}\text{alpha}$$

d)   After alpha (or beta) decay, a nucleus often has too much energy. How does it lose this energy?

....

Q7   Neutrons are very difficult to detect.

a)   Describe one way in which electrons can be detected.

....

b)   i)   Why is it not possible to detect neutrons in this way? ....

     ii)   How are neutrons detected?

       ....

Q8   Shielding made of **concrete** can be used as protection against neutron radiation.

a)   What type of nuclei is best for absorbing neutron radiation? ....

b)   Explain how the shielding works.

....

....

c)   Concrete shielding alone is not enough to prevent the harmful effects of neutron radiation. Explain why.

....

....

d)   Write down an example of a material that could be added to the shielding to stop any radiation getting through.

....

Fundamental and Other Particles

Q1   Many particles can be split into even smaller particles.

a)   What is a **fundamental particle**?

....

b)   Which of the following are fundamental particles?

| Proton | Electron | Neutron | Monkey | Positron | Alpha particle |

c)   Can new fundamental particles ever be created? How?

....

Q2   Tick the statements that are **true**.

a)   Quarks are made up of protons and neutrons.   ☐

b)   The relative mass of a quark is 1/3.   ☐

c)   All quarks have the same charge.   ☐

d)   There are 2 quarks in a proton.   ☐

e)   There are 2 types of quark in a neutron.   ☐

quark quark

Q3   Match the **particles** on the left with the correct description of their properties.

Electron

Down-quark

Proton

Neutron

Positron

Up-quark

relative mass 1/3, relative charge 2/3

relative mass 1, charge +1

fundamental particle, charge –1

relative charge –1/3

made up of two down-quarks and one up-quark

fundamental particle, charge +1

Q4   The number of protons and neutrons in a nucleus can make it **unstable**.

a)   Complete the following sentence.

To become more stable, the nucleus can convert a neutron into a ....

b)   What particle must be emitted to keep the overall charge zero? ....

c)   What is this process called? ....

Fundamental and Other Particles

Q5 Scientists at CERN carry out experiments involving smashing particles together at high speed.

a) Fill in the **gaps** in this passage.

> In an experiment, two protons are .... to very high speed and
>
> made to collide. The collision produces a large amount of ....
>
> Some of this .... can be turned into mass. The mass created is
>
> equal parts .... and anti..................................... .

b) Antimatter is made up of antiparticles

  i) Give one **similarity** between a particle and its antiparticle. ....

  ii) Give one **difference** between a particle and its antiparticle. ....

  iii) Name the antiparticle of the electron. ....

c) The **antiproton** is the antiparticle of the proton. Is the antiproton a fundamental particle?
Explain your answer.

....

d) What is the relative **charge** on an antiproton? ....

Q6 The charges on protons and neutrons are determined by the quarks that form them.

a) Make simple sketch diagrams of a **proton** and a **neutron**, showing the number and type of quarks
each contains.

Proton	Neutron

b) Complete the blanks in this sentence:

In beta decay, a proton is converted to a .... and a .... is emitted.

c) Describe β⁺ **decay** in terms of what happens to the quarks in a proton.

....

Top Tips: Everything, everywhere is made of particles — make sure you know each type,
their charge and mass. Learn which are fundamental, and how they go together to make the rest.

Electron Beams

Q1 The diagram shows an **electron gun**.

a) Use the following words to fill in the labels on the diagram. Words may be used more than once.

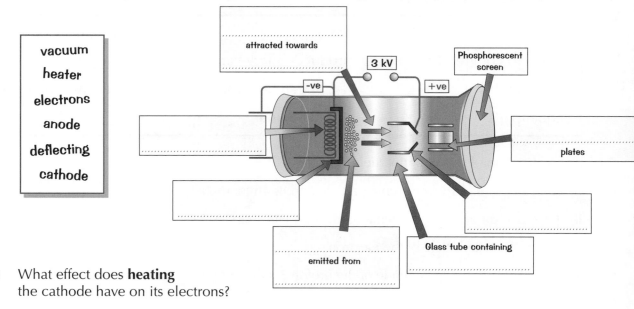

vacuum
heater
electrons
anode
deflecting
cathode

b) What effect does **heating** the cathode have on its electrons?

....

c) Which components in the electron gun use electric fields to make electrons change:

i) speed? ....

ii) direction? ....

d) What happens when an electron hits the phosphorescent screen?

....

Q2 A beam of electrons leaves an **electron gun**. The current carried by the beam is 4 mA.

a) What is current a measure of?

....

b) How many **coulombs** of charge pass a certain point in the beam per second?

....

c) How many **electrons** pass this point per second?

....

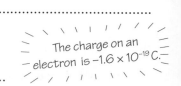
The charge on an electron is -1.6×10^{-19} C.

Q3 The electron beam in a cathode ray tube is deflected by an **electric field** between two pairs of charged metal plates. Circle the correct words from each pair to complete the following sentences.

a) The electron beam is **attracted to** / **repelled by** a positive charge and **attracted to** / **repelled by** a negative charge.

b) The **Y-plates** / **X-plates** deflect the beam up and down, while the **Y-plates** / **X-plates** deflect the beam left and right.

Electron Beams

Q4 An **electron** accelerates across a potential difference (voltage) of 4 kV.
The charge on the electron is -1.6×10^{-19} C.

a) Calculate the **kinetic energy** gained by the electron.

....

b) How much **potential energy** will the electron lose?

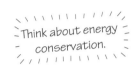

Think about energy conservation.

....

Q5 The diagram below shows the screen of an **oscilloscope**. The position of the spot of light is controlled by charged metal plates that **deflect** the beam of electrons from the cathode ray tube.

The dot shows the position of the electron beam when a positive potential is connected to X1 and Y1, so X1 is more positive than X2 and Y1 is more positive than Y2.

a) Draw in the position of the electron beam if the connections to X1 and X2 are swapped round so that a positive potential is connected to X2 and Y1.

b) Sketch the path of the electron beam from the point marked with a cross, as the following voltage changes occur:

i) The positive potential of X2 is increased while the positive potential of Y2 is also increased.

ii) When the potentials of X1 and X2 are equal, the positive potential of Y2 is decreased, while the positive potential of X2 continues to increase.

iii) The voltage changes stop when the potentials of Y1 and Y2 are equal. At this point X2 is more positive than X1.

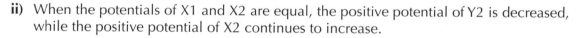

Q6 The diagram below shows a machine for taking **dental X-rays**.

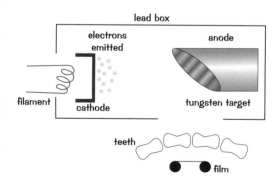

a) Sketch in and label the **path of the electron beam** on the diagram. Show the direction of the beam.

b) Sketch in and label the **path of the X-rays** on the diagram. Show the direction of the beam.

c) Why does the **electron beam** move from cathode to the anode?

....

....

d) At the **anode** the electrons from the beam strike atoms of tungsten, causing them to emit **X-rays**. Where does the energy for the X-rays come from?

....

P3 Topic 5 — Particles in Action

Electron Beams

Q7 Scientists at CERN use an enormous **particle accelerator** to smash particles into each other at tremendous speeds.

a) How are particle accelerators such as the one at CERN similar to electron guns?

....

The beams of charged particles in particle accelerators are deflected by charged metal plates in the same way as the beam of electrons in an electron gun.

b) When the factors below are **increased** will the deflection of a beam of charged particles increase, decrease or remain unchanged? Connect each factor with its effect on the deflection.

charge on the plates   increase   mass of the particles

mass of the plates   decrease

charge on the particles   no change   speed of the particles

c) Give two reasons why scientists from all over Europe collaborate on the research at CERN.

....

....

Q8 Laurence and Amy are experimenting with an **electron gun** similar to the one in question 1. They connect the anode and cathode with a wire containing an ammeter, as shown below.

a) The ammeter shows that a current is flowing even though there appears to be a gap in the circuit between the cathode and the anode. Describe how the circuit has been completed.

....

....

b) Laurence connects the positive terminal of a battery to the upper deflection plate, and the negative terminal of the battery to the lower deflection plate.

  i) What happens to the plates?

....

  ii) What happens to the electron beam?

....

  iii) What do they see on the phosphorescent screen?

....

c) Give a common 'household' use of electron guns. ....

Mixed Questions — P3 Topic 5

Q1 When **high-energy** electrons are fired at protons and neutrons the deflection of the electrons shows that both protons and neutrons are made up of charged particles called **quarks**.

   a) Describe the types of quark found in protons and neutrons, include their relative charge and mass.

      i) up-quarks: ....

      ii) down-quarks: ....

   b) Why do electrons **change direction** when they come near quarks?

      ....

Q2 Anna is investigating the properties of stable and unstable isotopes. She fires neutrons at a stable isotope of carbon. The isotope **absorbs a neutron** and becomes unstable. Anna adds the unstable isotope to a graph showing the number of neutrons and the number of protons in stable isotopes.

   a) Would you expect the unstable carbon isotope to lie above, below or on the line of stability on the graph? Give a reason for your answer.

      ....

   b) **i)** Complete the following equation describing the decay of the isotope: $^{13}_{6}C \longrightarrow \boxed{}_{\boxed{}}N + ^{0}_{-1}e$

      ii) What is this sort of decay called? ....

   c) Describe the decay in terms of what happens to the **quarks** in a neutron within the isotope's nucleus.

      ....

   d) The isotope is still unstable because it has too much **energy**. How can the isotope become stable?

      ....

Q3 A container of gas has a pressure of 1×10^5 N/m² and a volume of **100 cm³**.

   a) The volume of the gas is gradually increased while the temperature remains constant. Calculate the **pressure** of the gas at the following volumes.

      i) 200 cm³ ....

      ii) 400 cm³ ....

   b) When the pressure of the gas is 1.25×10^4 N/m², what will its **volume** be?

      ....

   c) On the grid opposite, draw a **graph** showing how pressure varies against volume at constant temperature for this gas.

74

Mixed Questions — P3 Topic 5

Q4 **Electron guns** are made up of many parts, each with its own specific function.

a) Draw lines to connect each part of the electron gun with its function.

X-plates

Deflection along a horizontal axis

Anode

Heats the cathode

Deflection along a vertical axis

Heater

Y-plates

Accelerates the electron beam

b) i) What is **thermionic emission**? ....

ii) Where in an electron gun does it occur? ....

A beam of electrons passes through an electric field generated by a pair of vertical deflector plates. The top plate is connected to the positive terminal of a battery, and the bottom plate is connected to the negative terminal.

upper deflector plate

☐ +

beam of particles →

☐ −

lower deflector plate

c) On the diagram, sketch the path the beam of electrons will take through the deflector plates.

d) Draw and label the paths you would expect a beam of the following particles to take through the deflector plates:

i) neutrons

ii) protons

e) It took 40 years from the discovery of protons and electrons for the neutron to be detected. Suggest a reason why the neutron was discovered so much later.

....

Q5 The gas inside a rigid, **sealed** container is cooled from 527 °C to –73 °C.

a) Convert these temperatures to kelvin:

i) 527 °C = ... K

ii) –73 °C = ... K

b) What will happen to:

i) the average **kinetic energy** of the gas particles? ....

ii) the average **speed** of the gas particles? ....

iii) the average **force** exerted on the walls of the container? ....

c) Use **kinetic theory** to explain how the pressure of a gas depends on the movement of particles.

....

....

d) What is the mathematical relationship between the kinetic energy and temperature of a gas?

....

P3 Topic 5 — Particles in Action

Mixed Questions — Topic 5

Q6   The **electron-volt (eV)** is the amount of kinetic energy gained by one electron when it moves through a potential difference of one volt.

a)   The charge on an electron is -1.6×10^{-19} C. What is the value, in joules, of 1 eV?

....

b)   Complete the blanks in the following passage:

Particle accelerators are used to make particles .... with each other at

high speed, releasing .... In some cases this ....

turns into ...., creating a particle / antiparticle pair.

c)   Why do physicists sometimes measure the mass of particles in eV?

....

d)   Apart from particle accelerators, suggest one other **scientific** use of electron guns.

....

Q7   Choose the correct **particle** or particles for each of the descriptions below. The same option may be used once, more than once or not at all.

protons   neutrons   ions   electrons   positrons

a)   can make up an electric current ....

b)   are fundamental particles ....

c)   are released in beta-plus decay ....

d)   are made up of three quarks ....

Q8   Radon gas is a source of background radiation that occurs naturally in the air.

a)   The following incomplete equation shows the decay of radon gas to solid polonium. $^{222}_{86}\text{Rn} \longrightarrow \boxed{}\text{Po} + \boxed{}$ ....

i)   What sort of decay would you expect radon to undergo? Give a reason for your answer.

....

ii)   Complete the equation.

b)   A rigid, sealed container of radon gas at a pressure of 101 kPa is heated from 273 K to 293 K. Calculate the pressure at the new temperature. Assume the radon behaves as an ideal gas.

....

....

Total Internal Reflection

Q1   The diagram shows light entering a glass block. Light travels **more slowly** in **glass** than in air.

Complete the diagram to show the ray passing through the block and emerging from the other side.
Include labels A to E for:

A   the refracted ray

B   the emergent ray

C   the normal for the emergent ray

D   the angle of incidence

E   the angle of refraction

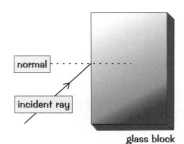

Q2   Choose from the words below to complete the passage.

| pulses | thousands | reflected | internal | diffraction | dense | core | infrared | gamma |

Optical fibres depend on total .... reflection for their operation.

Visible light or .... waves are sent down the cable and are

.... when they hit the boundary between the .... of the

fibre and the less .... outer case. The signals travel as ....

of light. Each cable can carry .... of different signals.

Q3   Tick to show whether these statements are **true** or **false**.

True False

a)   For the signal to be transmitted, the rays must not enter the fibre at too sharp an angle.   ☐ ☐

b)   Optical fibres are subject to interference from other signals.   ☐ ☐

Q4   The diagrams show rays of light in an **optical fibre**.
Draw arrows to match each diagram to the correct description of what is happening.

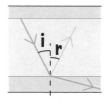

Total internal reflection

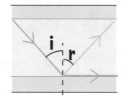

Most of the light passes out
of the optical fibre, but
some is reflected internally.

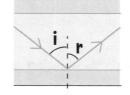

Most of the light is reflected
internally, but some emerges
along the surface of the glass.

Q5   What is meant by the '**critical angle**' for a material?

....

....

Medical Uses of Light

Q1   The diagram below shows a **pulse oximeter** on a hospital patient's **finger**.

a)   Add arrows to the diagram to show the direction of the red light and infrared beams.

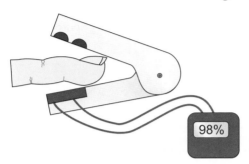

b)   Choose from the words given below to complete the passage about how a pulse oximeter works.

reflected	reduced	absorbed	calibrated	monkey	tissue	increased

Red and infrared light pass through the .... and are detected by a photo

detector. Some of the light is .... by the red blood so that the amount of

light detected by the detector is .... The amount of light absorbed depends

on the amount of oxyhaemoglobin in the blood so the display can be ....

to show the blood's oxyhaemoglobin content.

c)   State one other suitable part of the **body** where a pulse oximeter could be placed.
Explain your answer.

....

....

Q2   Optical fibres work because of repeated **total internal reflections**.

You'll need to measure the angle of incidence for each one — carefully.

a)   Complete the **ray diagrams** below. The critical angle for glass/air is **42°**.

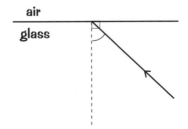

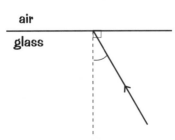

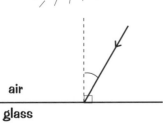

b)   What two conditions are essential for **total internal reflection** to occur?

1. ....

2. ....

Medical Uses of Light

Q3 Doctors use **endoscopes** to look inside patients' bodies. Endoscopes work using **optical fibres**.

a) What **material** could the optical fibres in an endoscope be made from?

....

b) Explain why doctors try not to to **bend** an endoscope sharply.

....

....

Q4 The diagram shows the use of an **endoscope** in **keyhole surgery**.

a) Explain what is meant by the term **keyhole surgery**.

....

....

b) Outline how an **endoscope** works.

....

....

c) List two **advantages** of keyhole surgery over conventional surgery.

....

Q5 **Reflection** pulse oximetry is used to measure the amount of oxygen in the blood.

a) How does reflection pulse oximetry differ from the type of pulse oximetry described in question 1?

....

b) Connect the boxes below to complete the sentences about haemoglobin.

Oxyhaemoglobin is...   ...purply coloured...   ...and doesn't contain much oxygen.

Reduced haemoglobin is...   ...bright red...   ...and rich in oxygen.

Top Tips: When you're learning about endoscopes, impress your friends by casually dropping the word 'esophagogastroduodenoscopy' into conversation. It means using an endoscope to have a look all the way down someone's throat right to their guts – mmm, nice.

Work, Power and Energy

Q1 In his new job, John has to climb the stairs on average **6 times** every day. After doing this for six months, he finds he has lost **15 kg**.

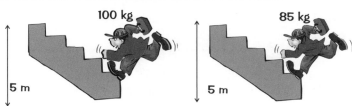

Calculate the work done by John each day in climbing the stairs:

a) When he started his new job.

....

b) Six months later, after his weight loss.

....

Q2 Kat was in a car accident and injured her left arm. Her physiotherapist gives Kat exercises to restore the power of her arm. For one exercise, Kat must **raise** a **100 N** load over **0.5 m**.

a) What is the work done by Kat in raising the load?

....

b) Complete the physiotherapist's table recording Kat's progress over four days of treatment.

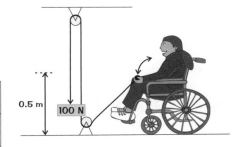

days of treatment	1	2	3	4
time taken to raise load (s)	5.0	4.0	....	1
patient's power rating (W)	10.0	....	20.0	....

c) What does Kat's changing power rating suggest about her arm?

....

d) What **further information** does the physiotherapist need if she is to decide whether or not Kat has fully recovered the power of her injured arm?

....

Q3 Isaac is stacking a **1.5 m** high shelf with **10 N** bags of sugar from the floor.

a) Calculate how much **energy** Isaac **transfers** to each bag.

....

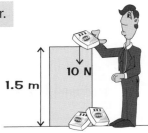

b) Calculate how much **work** Isaac does when he stacks 20 bags of sugar.

....

c) Is work a type of energy? Explain your answer.

....

Work, Power and Energy

Q4   Tim is canoeing down a stretch of river. Tim's mass is **73 kg** and his canoe weighs **190 N**.

a)   The river is flowing at 1.3 m/s. Tim starts off with the same speed as the river then paddles hard, accelerating to 4.4 m/s over 5 s. Calculate his acceleration.

....

b)   Tim accelerates at this rate over a distance of 150 m.
Calculate the work done by Tim on this part of the river.

....

....

Q5   Farmer Ted's horse can pull a load of **1000 N** over **20 m** in **25 s**.

a)   Calculate the power of Farmer Ted's horse.

....

b)   When he is not pulling a load, Farmer Ted's horse can run at 13 m/s. The mass of the horse is 800 kg. Calculate the **kinetic energy** gained by the horse when it accelerates from 0 to 13 m/s.

....

c)   Calculate the power, in **watts**, of the horse when it runs at 13 m/s for 90 s.

....

d)   Suggest a reason why the horse's power is lower in your second calculation.

....

Q6   Fiona is a weightlifter. She lifts a **70 kg barbell** from the floor to above her head, so it is **2.1 m** above the ground.

$g = 10\,m/s^2$

a)   How much potential energy has Fiona transferred to the barbell?

....

b)   If Fiona takes 5 s to lift the barbell how powerful is she?

....

c)   Fiona attempts to lift an 80 kg barbell. It takes her 5 s to get it to 1.9 m above the ground, but she cannot lift it any further, so drops the barbell to the floor.

i)   Calculate the power Fiona used in this lift.

....

ii)   Calculate the maximum velocity reached by the barbell as it falls. Ignore air resistance.

....

Energy and Metabolic Rate

Q1 The table shows some activities and the **metabolic rates** associated with them.

a) What does metabolic rate mean?

....

....

Activity	kJ/min
Sleeping	4.5
Watching TV	
Cycling (15 mph)	21
Jogging (5 mph)	40
Slow walking	14

b) Complete the table by inserting a suitable metabolic rate for **watching TV**.

c) i) Suggest three processes within a person's body that require energy while they're watching TV.

....

ii) Where does the energy for these processes come from?

....

Q2 Ed says that his metabolic rate must be lowest just after lunch because this is when he has the most trouble paying attention in lessons, so his body must be transferring energy to his brain very slowly.

a) Explain why Ed's reasoning is incorrect.

....

b) A person's lowest metabolic rate is called the **basal metabolic rate** or BMR.

i) What does BMR measure in terms of the processes going on in a person's body?

....

ii) Outline how to measure Ed's BMR and show him that his metabolic rate is higher after lunch.

....

....

....

Q3 The diagram shows Denny jogging up a hill. His metabolic rate as he jogs is **50 kJ/min**.

a) How much energy does Denny use in the 3 minutes it takes him to jog up the hill?

....

b) Calculate the potential energy Denny gains by reaching the top of the hill.

....

c) Explain why the energy used by Denny to jog up the hill is greater than the potential energy he gains at the top.

100 m

600 N

....

....

Energy and Metabolic Rate

Q4   The graph below shows how the **basal metabolic rate** of Joanna and her mum vary over time.

    a)   Joanna is 6 years old and her mum is 34. Use your knowledge of how BMR varies with **age** to label the graph. Use **J** for Joanna and **M** for her mum.

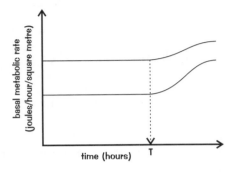

    b)   The graph shows that both Joanna and her mum's BMRs began to rise at time T.

        i)   Suggest what may have happened at **time T** to cause this.

        ....

        ii) What physical factor may have caused Joanna and her mum's BMRs to increase at different rates, as shown by the graph?

        ....

Q5   Chloe's doctor advises her that her current weight is unhealthy and she should try to lose some weight. Her friend suggests she should reduce her food consumption to 300 kcal per day.

    a)   **i)**   Explain the effect such a dramatic reduction in energy intake would have on Chloe's BMR.

        ....

        ii) Why would this not help Chloe lose as much weight as she might expect?

        ....

    b)   Chloe's doctor tells her that reducing her energy intake this much is a really bad way to lose weight, and could be harmful. He says she should start exercising as well as changing her eating habits. Give **two** reasons why exercise can help people to lose weight.

    ....

    ....

Q6   Dr Mayer worked with patients who travelled between Europe and Indonesia in the 20th century. He realised that his patients had a lower metabolic rate when they were in Indonesia than they had in Europe.

Explain how the difference between the European and tropical Indonesian climates caused this effect.

....

....

Electricity and the Body

Q1 Sharma is in hospital to have an **electromyogram** (**EMG**) of the muscles in her legs.
The muscles have become weaker recently, her doctor thinks she may have **muscular dystrophy**.

a) What does an EMG machine measure?

....

b) Define the following terms:

i) resting potential ....

ii) action potential ....

c) What value would you expect to record from a **contracted** muscle cell in a healthy person?

....

Q2 Electrocardiographs (ECGs) are used to measure the activity of the **heart**.

a) Describe, briefly, the **structure** of the heart.

....

b) Describe how a series of electrical signals help to produce a heart beat.

....

....

c) Describe the sensors used to detect the action potentials of a patient's heart.

....

Q3 The diagram below shows a typical **ECG**.

a) Show the size of the **resting potential** with an arrow on the y-axis.

b) What is the **period** of the heartbeat? ....

c) Calculate the frequency of the heartbeat in **beats per minute.**

....

d) What **muscle action** in the heart is being recorded at points:

i) P ....

ii) QRS ....

iii) T ....

Intensity of Radiation

Q1 The word '**radiation**' is often used to refer to nuclear sources, but it also covers many other types.

a) Sort the following forms of radiation according to their properties.

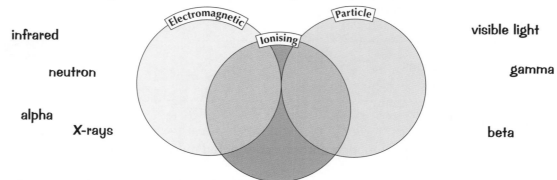

infrared   visible light

neutron   gamma

alpha
X-rays   beta

b) What is the definition of radiation?

....

Q2 Jonny is watching Kill Phil using a projector and a screen. The bulb in his projector gives an intensity of **8 W/m²** on the projector screen in its current position.

a) Write down the intensity of radiation on the screen if the distance between the bulb and screen is:

i) doubled. ....

ii) halved. ....

iii) quadrupled. ....

b) Write down the intensity of radiation on the screen if only the power of the bulb was doubled.

....

Q3 Sam and Amy have made a spherical lantern for the halloween parade. The lantern has a **diameter** of **40 cm** and contains a candle with a power of **0.8 W** at its center.

a) Calculate the surface area of the lantern, in square metres.

....

....

Remember the surface area of a sphere =4/3 π r²

b) Calculate the **intensity** of the light radiation on the inside surface of the lantern.

....

c) How will the intensity of the light from the candle reaching the outside surface of the lantern compare to that reaching the inside surface? Explain your answer.

....

Top Tips: If this intensity of radiation malarkey is just not making sense, try getting a torch out and seeing it in action. Hold your hand up close to the torch, what do you see — a bright spot of light. Shine it on the fence at the bottom of the garden, guess what — a large patch of dim light.

Nuclear Bombardment

Q1 Uranium-235 is split in nuclear reactors to release energy. Some products of the fission can also be used for medical applications.

a) Uranium-235 must be converted to uranium-236 using a thermal neutron.

  i) What is a thermal neutron?

  ....

  ii) Describe how uranium-235 is converted into uranium-236.

  ....

b) U-236 splits into two smaller atoms, which are often unstable. What makes these atoms unstable?

  ....

c) Suggest one medical application for the products of the fission of uranium-235.

  ....

Q2 Bombarding stable elements with **protons** can produce **radioactive isotopes**. Complete the following passage using the words provided.

nucleus	accelerator	cyclotron	electron	proton	element	mass

A proton is absorbed by the .... This increases its

.... number so a new .... is produced.

The proton needs a lot of energy before it can be absorbed by the nucleus, so this process

takes place in a particle .... called a ....

Q3 The radioisotopes produced by proton bombardment are **unstable**.

a) Complete the following equations to show how two radioisotopes are formed.

$$^{18}_{8}O + {}^{1}_{1}p \longrightarrow \boxed{}F + {}^{1}_{0}n \qquad ^{14}_{7}N + {}^{1}_{1}p \longrightarrow \boxed{}C + {}^{4}_{2}He$$

b) **i)** What sort of radiation do the radioisotopes formed in this way usually emit?

  ....

  ii) Suggest a medical use for these radioisotopes.

  ....

  iii) Explain why some hospitals have their own facilities for producing these radioisotopes.

  ....

Momentum Conservation

Q1 The diagram shows a fast moving **neutron colliding** with a stationary sodium **nucleus** and bouncing off again.

a) Using the notation in the diagram, write an expression for:

  i) the total momentum before the collision.

  ....

  ii) the total momentum after the collision.

  ....

b) Using your answers to part a), explain what is meant by the term **conservation of momentum**.

....

Q2 The diagram below shows the **collision** of a neutron and an atom of uranium-235.

Use the relative masses in your calculations.

a) Calculate the relative momentum of the:

  i) neutron. ....

  ii) uranium-235 nucleus. ....

b) The uranium-235 nucleus absorbs the neutron to form uranium-236. What is the relative momentum of the uranium-236 isotope?

....

Q3 The diagram shows the **alpha decay** of **uranium-238**.

a) **i)** Add an arrow to the diagram to show which way the **thorium** nucleus will move.

  ii) Explain why it must move this way.

  ....

b) Calculate the **velocity** of the thorium nucleus immediately after the decay.

....

Q4 A **proton** collides with a **stationary** isotope of **oxygen-16** and is absorbed.

a) The collision forms an isotope of fluorine with a relative mass of 17 and a velocity of 37 km/s.

  i) Calculate the relative momentum of the fluorine atom after the collision.

  ....

  ii) What was the velocity of the proton before the collision?

  ....

b) The fluorine isotope is unstable and emits an alpha particle at a velocity of –15 000 km/s. What is the velocity of the nitrogen-13 isotope formed by this decay?

....

Momentum Conservation

Q5 The diagram represents the **collision** of an **electron** and a **positron**.

electron   positron

a) What is the result of a collision between a particle and its antiparticle?

....

b) The electron and positron are travelling at the same speed before the collision. What is the value of their **total momentum** immediately before the collision?

....

c) Choose the correct words from each pair to complete the sentences below.

The collision of an electron and a positron produces a pair of **gamma rays** / **radioactive particles**. The **gamma rays** / **radioactive particles** produced have the same **energy** / **velocity** as each other, and opposite **energies** / **velocities**.

d) Explain how this collision is an example of mass/energy conservation.

....

....

Q6 A proton with a velocity of -2 km/s is travelling towards an electron moving at 90 km/s.

a) In box A, sketch a diagram showing the proton and the electron just before they collide.

A	B

b) The mass of an electron is approximately 1/2000th the mass of a proton. Calculate the total relative momentum just before the particles collide.

....

c) Just after the collision the electron has a velocity of -3000 km/s. Calculate the velocity of the proton immediately after the collision.

....

d) In box B, draw a diagram to show the particles immediately after the collision.

Top Tips: If you know your equations, this section is the chance to earn some tasty marks without too much trouble. Learning equations isn't the most exciting job in the world — but it does pay off. Remember, things with momentum are **mo_v_ing** — and that momentum equation — m × v.

Medical Uses of Radiation

Q1 **Positron emission tomography** (PET) is a scanning technique used in hospitals.

   a) Give one advantage and one disadvantage of PET compared to X-rays.

     i) advantage: ....

     ii) disadvantage: ....

   b) Give two conditions that can be researched using PET.

     ....

Q2 Put the following stages in the right order to explain how PET is carried out.

   ☐ The radiotracer moves through the body to the organs.

   ☐ Detectors around the body record the position of the emitted gamma rays.

   ☐ The patient is injected with the radiotracer.

   ☐ The positrons collide with electrons and are annihilated, releasing gamma rays.

   ☐ The radioisotope emits positrons.

   1 A positron-emitting radioactive isotope is added to a substance used by the body to make a radio tracer.

   ☐ A computer builds up a map of radioactivity in the body.

Q3 The **map of radioactivity** in the body produced by a PET scan can be used to detect active cancer tumors.

   a) **i)** What does the map of radioactivity match up with?

     ....

     ii) Why is this?

     ....

   b) Explain why a PET scan is a good way to detect cancer.

     ....

   c) Why is PET not used frequently on the same patient?

     ....

Q4 **Radiation exposure** can be damaging, but is also used as a medical treatment.

   a) Explain how radiotherapy can be used as a form of **palliative care**.

     ....

     ....

   b) Describe **two** ways that radiation can damage cells.

     ....

Medical Research

Q1 Draw lines to match each medical **technique** on the left to the medical **condition** or process each might be used in.

Endoscope

ECG

PET

Antibiotic development

Keyhole surgery

Monitoring heart conditions

Mutating bacteria ('superbugs')

Locating cancer cells

Q2 Imagine a new drug has been developed to treat breast cancer. It has been tested on people with end-stage breast cancer, and shown to be an effective treatment with tolerable side effects.

a) The drug has not been tested on people with early-stage breast cancer.

   i) Why might someone with early-stage breast cancer want to take this drug?

   ....

   ii) Suggest why doctors would be unwilling to give this drug to patients with early-stage breast cancer.

   ....

b) An alternative treatment for breast cancer is radiotherapy. However, there are environmental issues, as well as unpleasant side effects, associated with radiotherapy. Outline one such issue.

....

Q3 Read the following extract from a newspaper article about a drug trial.

> Six men are tonight in a critical condition in hospital after taking part in a drug trial. The drug being tested was intended to treat chronic inflammatory conditions and leukaemia, but has instead left these men fighting for their lives. A spokesperson for the drug company involved has stressed that they followed all procedures correctly, including carrying out extensive laboratory studies before these trials began.

a) What might the **laboratory studies** have been?

....

b) Suggest why the laboratory studies did not predict the severe reaction seen in the patients.

....

....

c) Give one **positive outcome** of this test.

....

Mixed Questions — P3 Topic 6

Q1 One of Dr McLeod's patients has cancer and is being treated with **radiotherapy**.

a) What sort of radiation would be used in this treatment?

....

b) Describe how radiotherapy can help treat cancer.

....

c) Dr McLeod thinks that the radiotherapy won't cure his patient's cancer, but will reduce her suffering. What type of care is this? ....

d) Dr McLeod hears about a new drug that might help his patient. The drug has not yet been tested on cancer patients and the company is looking for volunteers to take part in a trial. Outline an argument for and against this patient taking part in the trial.

For: ....

....

Against: ....

....

Q2 Mary has epilepsy. She is having a **PET scan** of her brain as part of a research study. The researcher injects Mary with a radiotracer before scanning her brain.

a) Describe what happens to the **positrons** emitted by the radiotracer in Mary's brain.

....

b) Explain how **momentum** is **conserved** in this process.

....

....

....

Q3 Nurse Horton uses a **pulse oximeter** to monitor the blood oxygen content of a patient who has recently had surgery.

a) Describe and explain how a pulse oximeter works.

....

....

b) If the blood has a high oxygen content, what colour will the oxyhaemoglobin appear?

....

Mixed Questions — P3 Topic 6

Q4 James's doctor thinks he may have a **cancerous tumour** in his intestine. James goes to hospital to have a PET scan of his abdomen.

a) Before the PET scan, James is given an **injection**. What would this contain?

....

b) The PET scan shows an area with much higher metabolic activity than the rest of the intestine. Could this area be **cancerous**? Explain your answer.

....

c) The surgeon decides to investigate further using keyhole surgery.

  i) Name the **instrument** the surgeon would use to see inside James's body. ....

  ii) The instrument contains **optical fibres** to carry light into James's body and an image back out. Describe how light is carried along an optical fibre.

  ....

  ....

d) During the operation James is connected to an **ECG** machine to monitor the activity of his heart.

  i) What does an ECG measure?

  ....

  ii) Sketch the shape of a typical ECG on the axes provided. Label the components of the curve.

(graph with axes labelled "p.d. at electrodes" and "time (s)")

e) The time from peak to peak on James' ECG is **0.75 s**. What is his heart rate in beats per minute?

....

Q5 Karen has hurt her foot playing football. She is having an **X-ray** to find out whether she has broken a bone.

a) The X-rays have an **intensity** of 430 W/m². The surface area of Karen's foot is 0.024 m². Calculate the approximate **power** of the radiation reaching Karen's foot.

....

b) What does 'radiation' mean?

....

c) Karen is given special glasses to wear while the X-ray is taken. Explain why.

....

....

d) The radiographer goes behind a lead screen while Karen has her X-ray. Why does he does this?

....

Mixed Questions — P3 Topic 6

Q6 An atom of nitrogen is bombarded with **proton radiation** in a cyclotron.

a) Why does this process need to take place in a cyclotron?

....

b) The nitrogen nucleus absorbs a proton. Why does this result in a new **element**?

....

c) The new element formed is an unstable isotope of carbon.
What sort of radiation would you expect it to emit?

....

Q7 Rob is using an EMG machine to measure the activity in the muscles of his arm when he lifts a **20 N** weight. He lifts the weight onto a shelf, a vertical distance of 0.45 m then relaxes his arm.

a) Explain how an EMG machine measures muscle activity.

....

b) Calculate the **work** Rob does in lifting the weight once.

....

c) Rob now performs a set of 10 lifts in 24 s. Calculate the **power** he has generated.

....

....

d) Name one medical condition that EMG scans can help to diagnose. ....

Q8 A uranium-235 nucleus is bombarded with neutron radiation and absorbs a **thermal neutron**.

a) Write a nuclear equation to represent uranium-235 absorbing a thermal neutron.

....

b) The new uranium isotope is unstable and splits into two smaller atoms and two neutrons.
The uranium isotope was **stationary** before the fission took place.

i) What is the total **mass** of the fission products (in atomic mass units)?

....

ii) What is their total **momentum**? Give a reason for your answer.

....